Thy Will Be Done

St. Francis de Sales

Thy Will Be Done
Letters to Persons in the World

SOPHIA INSTITUTE PRESS
Manchester, New Hampshire

Thy Will Be Done: Letters to Persons in the World draws on the English translation of the letters of St. Francis de Sales originally published in *The Library of St. Francis de Sales*, vol. 1, *Letters to Persons in the World*, translated by the Very Reverend Henry Benedict Mackey (London: Burns & Oates, Ltd.; New York, Cincinnati, Chicago: Benziger Brothers, 1894). For this 1995 edition, there have been extensive editorial revisions and improvements in the translation.

Jacket design by Joan Barger

Sophia Institute Press
Box 5284, Manchester, NH 03108
1-800-888-9344

Library of Congress Cataloging-in-Publication Data

Francis, de Sales, Saint, 1567-1622.
    [Correspondence. English. Selections]
    Thy will be done : letters to persons in the world / St. Francis
de Sales.
      p. cm.
    ISBN 0-918477-28-X. — ISBN 0-918477-29-8 (pbk.)
    1. Francis, de Sales, Saint, 1567-1622 — Correspondence.
2. Christian saints — Switzerland — Correspondence. 3. Spiritual
life — Catholic Church — Early works to 1800. I. Title.
BX4700.F85A4   1995
282' .092 — dc20
  [B]   95-13475 CIP

95 96 97 98 99 10 9 8 7 6 5 4 3 2 1

Table of Contents

Thy Will Be Done

Loving and Serving God
in Your Daily Life

Contents

Contents

Editor's Note: The biblical references in the following pages are based on the Douay-Rheims edition of the Old and New Testaments. Quotations from the Psalms and some of the historical books of the Bible have been cross-referenced with the differing names and enumeration in the Revised Standard Version, using the following symbol: (RSV =).

Foreword

by Alice von Hildebrand

In his holy *Rule*, St. Benedict writes of the abbot of the monastery: "Let him realize also how difficult and arduous a task he has undertaken, of ruling souls and adapting himself to many dispositions. One he must honor, another rebuke, another persuade, according to each one's disposition and understanding, and thus adapt and accommodate himself to all in such a way that he may not only suffer no loss in the sheep committed to him, but may even rejoice in the increase of a good flock."[1]

St. Francis de Sales was no abbot, but in addressing himself to the topic of how to choose a spiritual director, he warns souls that they cannot be careful enough in their selection, for the chances of finding a worthy and good one are very small indeed, one in thousands.

I wonder if he realized, when writing these words, that those under his guidance had truly found in him the precious pearl, one of the greatest spiritual directors in the history of

---

[1] *The Rule of Benedict*, ch. 2.

the Catholic Church. Maybe a few others were as great as he was; none was greater.

He guided innumerable souls from all walks of life, adapting himself to each individual mold, each individual rhythm, each individual need. He himself writes that souls differ more widely from each other than human faces do. He, no doubt, needed all the qualities that St. Benedict claims abbots should possess to tend this amazing variety of flowers in God's garden.

Yet St. Francis always kept in mind that however different souls might be, all of them ultimately have the same vocation: to glorify God by their holiness — that is, to be transformed in Christ. Endowed with natural grace, illumined by supernatural grace, St. Francis knew how to adapt himself to each individual case. With an intuitive sense that clearly came from above, he knew when to encourage, when to rebuke, when to moderate and slacken the pace of those anxious to run, when to quicken the pace of those who were sluggish. He combined patience and love with firmness in his principles, never deviating from the teaching of holy Church. He made no distinction of persons; to all his spiritual children, whether rich or poor, cultivated or uncouth, male or female, he gave the same loving care, the same unconditional devotion.

While feeling a holy envy for those souls to whom these letters were written, we can nevertheless benefit from his supernatural wisdom by reading and meditating on them. Their publication should be welcomed by all those who long to be helped on their way to God.

Prayer, Faith, and Accepting Your Vocation

"Thy will be done"

*To a young woman prevented
from becoming a nun*

Mademoiselle,

You should resign yourself entirely into the hands of the good God, who, when you have done your little duty about this inspiration and design that you have, will be pleased with whatever you do, even if it be much less. In a word, you must have courage to do everything to become a religious, since God gives you such a desire. But if after all your efforts you cannot succeed, you could not please our Lord more than by sacrificing to Him your will, and remaining in tranquillity, humility, and devotion, entirely conformed and submissive to His divine will and good pleasure. You will recognize this clearly enough when, having done your best, you cannot fulfil your desires.

For our good God sometimes tries our courage and our love, depriving us of the things that seem to us, and which really are, very good for the soul. And if He sees us ardent in their pursuit, and yet humble, tranquil, and resigned to doing without and

Thy Will Be Done

to the privation of the thing sought, He gives us blessings greater in the privation than in the possession of the thing desired. For in all things and everywhere, God loves those who with good heart and simplicity, on all occasions and in all events, can say to Him, "Thy will be done."[2]

Your humble servant,

Francis

[2] Matt. 6:10.

"Do the will of God joyfully"

To a woman, on obtaining
true devotion and peace of soul

Madame,

It has been an extreme pleasure to me to receive and read your letter. I should like mine to give you a return of pleasure, and particularly to remedy the disquietudes that have arisen in your spirit since our separation. God deign to inspire me.

I told you once, and I recall it very well, that I had found in your general confession all the marks of a true, good, and solid confession, and that I had never received one that had contented me so entirely. It is the truth, Madame, my dear sister, and be sure that on such occasions I speak very exactly.

If you have omitted to mention something, reflect whether this has been with knowledge and voluntarily; for in that case you must certainly make your confession again, if what you omitted was a mortal sin, or if you thought at the time that it was. But if it was only a venial sin, or if you omitted it through forgetfulness or lack of memory, do not be afraid, my dear sister. You are not bound — and I say this at the hazard of my soul — to make your confession again, but it will do to mention to your ordinary confessor the point you have left out. I answer for it.

Again, do not be afraid of not having used as much diligence as was required for your general confession; for I tell you again very clearly and confidently, that if you have made no voluntary omission you have no need at all to make again a confession that has really been very sufficiently made, so be at peace about that matter. And if you will discuss the matter with the Father Rector, he will tell you the same about it; for it is the sentiment of the Church our Mother.

The rules of the Rosary and the Cord[3] oblige one neither under mortal nor under venial sin, directly or indirectly; and if you do not observe them, you no more commit a sin than by omitting to do any other good work. Do not then distress yourself at all about them, but serve God joyfully with liberty of spirit.

You ask me what means you must use to gain devotion and peace of soul. My dear sister, you ask me no little thing; but I will try to tell you something about it, because my duty to you requires it. But take good notice of what I say.

The virtue of devotion is nothing other than a general inclination and readiness of the soul to do what it knows to be agreeable to God. It is that enlargement of heart of which David said, "I have run the way of Your commandments, when Thou didst enlarge my heart."[4]

---

[3] This refers to a type of confraternity, or pious society, whose members wore a cord or sash to honor some saint, from whom they hoped to receive a grace or favor.

[4] Ps. 118:32 (RSV = Ps. 119:32).

Do the will of God joyfully

Those who are simply good people walk in the way of God; but the devout run, and when they are very devout they fly. Now, I will tell you some rules that you must keep if you would be truly devout.

Before all it is necessary to keep the general command-ments of God and the Church, which are made for every faithful Christian. Without this there can be no devotion in the world. That, everyone knows.

Besides the general commandments, it is necessary care-fully to observe the particular commandments that each per-son has in regard to his vocation, and whoever does not observe this, if he should raise the dead, does not cease to be in sin and to be damned if he die in it. For example, it is commanded to bishops to visit their sheep — to teach, cor-rect, console. I may pass the whole week in prayer; I may fast all my life; if I do not do that, I am lost. If a person does miracles while in the state of marriage, but does not render the debt of marriage to his spouse[5] or does not concern himself with his children, "he is worse than an infidel";[6] and so with persons in other states of life.

These are the two sorts of commandments that we must carefully keep as the foundation of all devotion, and yet the virtue of devotion does not consist merely in observing them, but in observing them with readiness and willingly. Now, to gain this readiness we must consider several points.

The first is that God wills it so; and it is indeed reasonable that we should do His will, for we are in this world only for

[5] 1 Cor. 7:3-5.
[6] 1 Tim. 5:8.

that. Alas! Every day we ask Him that His will may be done; and when it comes to the doing, we have such difficulty! We offer ourselves to God so often; we say to Him at every step, "Lord, I am yours, here is my heart"; and when He wants to make use of us, we are so cowardly! How can we say we are His, if we are unwilling to accommodate our will to His?

The second consideration is to think of the nature of the commandments of God, which are mild, gracious, and sweet, not only the general commandments but also the particular ones of our vocation. And what is it, then, that makes them burdensome to you? Nothing, in truth, save your own will, which desires to reign in you at any cost. And the things that perhaps it would desire if they were not commanded, once they are commanded, it rejects.

Of a hundred thousand delicious fruits, Eve chose that which had been forbidden to her;[7] and doubtless if it had been allowed, she would not have eaten of it. The fact is, in a word, that we want to serve God, but after *our will*, and not after *His*.

Saul was commanded to spoil and ruin all he found in Amalek. He destroyed all, except what was precious; this he reserved, and offered in sacrifice. But God declared that He would have no sacrifice against obedience.[8] God commands me to help souls, yet I want to rest in contemplation. The contemplative life is good, but not in opposition to obedience. We are not to choose at our own will. We must wish what God wishes; and if God wishes me to serve Him in one thing, I ought not to wish to serve Him in another. God wishes Saul

---

[7] Gen. 3:1-6.

[8] 1 Kings 15:3:23 (RSV = 1 Sam. 15:3-23).

to serve Him as king and as captain, and Saul wishes to serve Him as priest.[9] There is no doubt that the latter is more excellent than the former; yet God does not care about that: He wants to be obeyed.

Just look at this! God had given manna to the children of Israel,[10] a very delicious meal, and lo! They will none of it, but, in their desires, seek after the garlic and onions of Egypt.[11] It is our wretched nature that always wishes its own will to be done and not the will of God. Now, in proportion as we have less of our own will, that of God is more easily observed.

We must consider that there is no vocation that has not its irksome aspects, its bitternesses, and disgusts. And what is more, except for those who are fully resigned to the will of God, each one would willingly change his condition for that of others: those who are bishops would like not to be; those who are married would like not to be, and those who are not married would like to be. Whence comes this general disquietude of souls, if not from a certain dislike of constraint and a perversity of spirit that makes us think that each one is better off than we?

But it all comes to the same: whoever is not fully resigned, let him turn himself here or there, he will never have rest. Those who have fever find no place comfortable; they have not stayed a quarter of an hour in one bed when they want to be in another. It is not the bed that is at fault, but the fever that everywhere torments them. A person who has not the

---

[9] 1 Kings 13:9-13 (RSV = 1 Sam. 13:9-13).

[10] Exod. 16:14-31.

[11] Num. 11:4-5.

fever of self-will is satisfied with everything, provided that God is served. He cares not in what capacity God employs him, provided that he does the divine will. It is all one to him.

But this is not all: we must not only will to do the will of God, but in order to be devout, we must do it joyfully. If I were not a bishop, knowing what I know, I should not wish to be one; but being one, not only am I obliged to do what this trying vocation requires, but I must do it joyously, and must take pleasure in it and be contented. It is the saying of St. Paul: "Let each one stay in his vocation before God."[12]

We do not have to carry the cross of others, but our own; and so that each may carry his own, our Lord wishes him to renounce himself — that is, his own will.[13] "I should like this or that"; "I should be better here or there": those are temptations. Our Lord knows well what He does. Let us do what He wills; let us stay where He has placed us.

But, my good daughter, allow me to speak to you according to my heart, for so I love you. You would like to have some little practice to regulate yourself by.

Besides what I have told you to reflect upon, every day — either in the morning before dinner, or an hour or two before supper — meditate on the life and death of our Lord; and for this purpose use Bellintani the Capuchin,[14] or Bruno the Jesuit.[15] Your meditation should last only a good half hour, and

---

[12] 1 Cor. 7:24.

[13] Matt. 16:24.

[14] Mattia da Salò Bellintani (1534-1611), a Capuchin preacher and spiritual writer, author of a book on the practice of mental prayer.

[15] Bruno Vincent (1532-1594), Italian Jesuit, author of *Meditations on the Mysteries of the Passion and Resurrection of Jesus Christ our Lord*.

not more. At the end of it add always a consideration of the obedience that our Lord showed toward God His Father. For you will find that all He has done, He did to fulfil the will of His Father, and by reflection on this try to gain for yourself a great love of the will of God.

Before doing, or preparing to do, things in your vocation that are trials to you, recall that the saints have joyfully done things far greater and harder: some have suffered martyrdom, others the dishonor of the world. St. Francis and many religious of our age have kissed and kissed again a thousand times those afflicted with leprosy and ulcers; others have confined themselves to the deserts; others to the galleys with soldiers; and all this to do what pleases God. And what do we do that approaches in difficulty to this?

Think often that all we do has its true value from our conformity with the will of God, so that in eating and drinking, if I do it because it is the will of God for me to do it, I am more agreeable to God than if I suffer death without that intention.

I would wish you often, during the day, to ask God to give you love of your vocation, and to say like St. Paul when he was converted, "Lord, what will You have me to do?"[16] Will You have me serve You in the vilest ministry of Your house? Ah! I shall consider myself too happy. Provided that I serve You, I do not care in what it may be. And coming to the particular thing that troubles you, say, "Will You that I do such a thing? Ah! Lord, although I am not worthy to do it, I will do it most willingly," and thus you greatly humble yourself. Oh my God!

[16] Acts 9:6.

11

What a treasure you will gain! One greater, without doubt, than you can imagine.

I would wish you to consider how many saints have been in your vocation and state, and how they have accommodated themselves to it with great sweetness and resignation, both under the New and the Old Testaments. Sara, Rebecca, St. Anne, St. Elizabeth, St. Monica, St. Paula, and a hundred thousand others; and let this encourage you, recommending yourself to their prayers.

We must love what God loves. Now, He loves our vocation; so let us also love it, and not occupy ourselves with thinking on that of others. Let us do our duty; each one's cross is not too much for him.

Mingle sweetly the office of Martha with that of Magdalen; do diligently the service of your vocation, and often recollect yourself, and put yourself in spirit at the feet of our Lord, and say, "My Lord, whether I run or stay, I am all Yours and You mine: You are my first spouse; and whatever I do is for love of You, both this and that". . . .

I think that, making half an hour's prayer every morning, you should content yourself with hearing one Mass a day, and reading during the day for half an hour some spiritual book, such as Granada[17] or some other good author.

In the evening make an examination of conscience, and all the day long, spontaneous prayers. Often read the *Spiritual Combat*; I recommend it to you.[18] On Sundays and feasts, you

[17] Luis de Granada (1504-1588), Spanish Dominican, author of the very popular *Guide for Sinners* and other books.

[18] *The Spiritual Combat*, a favorite book of St. Francis, first appeared anonymously in Venice in 1589.

can, besides Mass, hear Vespers (but not under obligation) and the sermon.

Do not forget to confess every week, and also when you have any great trouble of conscience. As for Communion, if it is not agreeable to Monsieur your husband, do not exceed, for the present, the limits of what we fixed at Saint Claude: keep steadfast, and receive Communion spiritually. God will take, as sufficient for the present, the preparation of your heart.

Remember what I have often said to you: do honor to your devotion; make it very amiable to all those who may know you, especially to your family; act so that every one may speak well of it. My God! How happy you are to have a husband so reasonable and so compliant! You should indeed praise God for this.

When any contradiction comes upon you, thoroughly resign yourself unto our Lord, and console yourself, knowing that His favors are only for the good or for those who put themselves in the way of becoming so.

For the rest, know that my spirit is all yours. God knows if ever I forget you, or your whole family, in my weak prayers; I have you deeply graven in my soul. May God be your heart and your life!

Francis

· "Serve God where you are"

To a priest, on fidelity to one's calling

My very dear confrère,

Pardon me, I beg you, for taking so long to respond to the first letter you ever wrote to me; it will not be so with the others, if I have the consolation of receiving any. But I was so occupied with my departure that I did not have any sort of leisure with which to render to you this duty; and, with that, I placed my hope in your affection, that you would interpret the delay benevolently.

I persist always in telling you that you must serve God where you are and do what you are doing. Not, my dear brother, that I would like to hinder the increase of your good spiritual exercises or the continual purification of your heart; but continue to do what you are doing, and better than you are doing it. Because I know well that God commands all His faithful in the person of Abraham, "Walk before me, and be perfect";[19] I also know that "blessed are those who walk in the

---

[19] Gen. 17:1.

ways" of the Lord,[20] that our fathers walked in them, and that they "resolved to ascend by steps," so that they might go from "virtue to virtue."[21]

Therefore have good courage to cultivate this vineyard, contributing your little effort to the spiritual good of the souls that the Lord has reserved for Himself lest they "bend their knees before Baal,"[22] "in the midst of a people that has unclean lips."[23] Do not be surprised if the fruits do not yet appear, because if you do the work of God patiently, your labor will not be "in vain in the Lord."[24]

Alas! Sir, God has nourished us with the gentle milk of many consolations so that, having grown up, we might try to help in the rebuilding of the walls of Jerusalem, whether by carrying stones, or by mixing the mortar, or by hammering. Believe me, remain there where you are; do faithfully everything in good conscience that morally you can do, and you will see that "if you believe, you will see the glory of God."[25] And if indeed you wish to do well, consider as temptation everything that will be suggested to you regarding changing your place; because as long as your spirit looks elsewhere than where you are, it will never apply itself rightly to profiting from where you are.

Well, know that all this has been said in the confidence that you gave me in your letter, and in the sincere friendship

[20] Ps. 127:1 (RSV = Ps. 128:1).

[21] Ps. 83:6, 8 (RSV = Ps. 84:5, 7).

[22] 3 Kings 19:18 (RSV = 1 Kings 19:18).

[23] Isa. 6:5.

[24] 1 Cor. 15:58.

[25] John 11:40.

that I bear for you in the bosom of the One whose side was pierced for love of us. I entreat Him that He may strengthen more and more in you the zeal of His honor, and I am with all my heart,

Your humble and very affectionate servant,

Francis

4

"Let us be what we are, and let us be it well"

*To a wife who thinks
marriage hinders holiness*

Madame my dearest sister,

You see me in readiness to write to you, and I know not what to say, except to tell you to walk always joyfully in this heavenly way in which God has placed you. I will bless Him all my life for the graces He has prepared for you; prepare for Him, on your part, as an acknowledgment, great resignations, and courageously lead your heart to the execution of the things you know He wants from you, in spite of all kinds of contradictions that might oppose themselves to this.

Regard not at all the substance of the things you do, but the honor they have, however trifling they may be, to be willed by our God, to be ordered by His Providence, and to be disposed by His wisdom. In a word, being agreeable to God, and recognized as such, to whom can they be disagreeable?

Be attentive, my dearest child, to make yourself every day more pure of heart. This purity consists in estimating and weighing all things in the balance of that sanctuary, which is nothing other than the will of God.

Love nothing too much, not even virtues, which are lost sometimes by passing the bounds of moderation. I do not know whether you understand me, but I think so: I refer to your desires, your ardors. It is not the property of roses to be white, I think — for the red are lovelier and of sweeter smell — but it is the property of lilies.

Let us be what we are, and let us be it *well*, to do honor to the Master whose work we are. People laughed at the painter, who wishing to represent a horse, painted a perfect bull. The work was fine in itself, but of little credit to the workman, who had another design, and had done well by chance.

Let us be what God likes, so long as we are His, and let us not be what we want to be, if it is against His intention. For if we were the most excellent creatures under Heaven, what would it profit us if we were not according to the pleasure of God's will? Perhaps I repeat this too much; but I will not say it so often again, as our Lord has already strengthened you much in this point.

Do me this pleasure, to let me know the subject of your meditations for the present year. I shall be consoled to know it, and also the fruit they produce in you. Rejoice in our Lord, my dear sister, and keep your heart in peace. I salute your husband, and am forever, Madame,

Your affectionate and faithful brother,

Francis

5

"Our faith should be naked and simple"

To a nun, on Christian faith

My dearest child,

. . . The truths of the Faith are sometimes agreeable to the human spirit, not only because God has revealed them by His word and proposed them by His Church, but also because these truths suit our taste, and because we enter into them thoroughly, we understand them easily, and they are according to our inclinations.

Consider, for example, the fact that there is a Paradise after this mortal life. This is a truth of the Faith that many hold much to their satisfaction, because it is sweet and desirable. That God is merciful the greatest part of the world finds to be a very good thing, and easily believes, because even philosophy teaches us this; it is conformable both to our taste and to our desire.

Now, not all the truths of the Faith are of this kind; consider, for example, the fact that there is an eternal Hell for the punishment of the wicked. This is a truth of the Faith, but a bitter, terrifying, fearful truth, and one that we do not willingly believe, except by the force of God's word.

And now I say first, that naked and simple faith is that by which we believe the truths of the Faith, without considering any pleasure, sweetness, or consolation we may have in them, but solely by the acquiescence of our spirit in the authority of the word of God and the proposition of the Church. And thus we believe the terrifying truths no less than the sweet and agreeable truths. Then our faith is naked, because it is not clothed with any sweetness or any relish; and it is simple, because it is not mingled with any satisfaction of our own feelings.

Secondly, there are truths of the Faith that we can apprehend by the imagination: for example, that our Lord was born in the manger of Bethlehem, that He was carried into Egypt, that He was crucified, that He went up to Heaven. On the other hand, there are others, which we cannot at all grasp with the imagination: for example, the truth of the most holy Trinity, eternity, the presence of our Lord's body in the most holy sacrament of the Eucharist. For all these truths are true in a way that is inconceivable to our imagination, since we cannot imagine *how* these things can be. Still, our understanding believes them firmly and simply, on the sole assurance it has of the word of God. And this faith is truly naked, for it is divested of all imagination; and it is entirely simple, because it has no sort of action except the action of our understanding, which purely and simply embraces these truths on the sole security of God's word. This faith, thus naked and simple, is that which the saints have practiced and continue to practice amid sterilities, drynesses, distrusts, and darknesses.

Faith should be simple

To live in truth — and not in untruth — is to lead a life entirely conformed to naked and simple faith according to the operations of grace and not of nature. This is because our imagination, our senses, our feeling, our taste, our consolations, and our arguments may be deceived and may err. To live according to them is to live in untruth, or at least in a perpetual risk of untruth; but to live in naked and simple faith — this is to live in truth.

So it is said of the wicked spirit, that "he abode not in the truth."[26] Having had faith in the beginning of his creation, he left it, wishing to contend, without the Faith, about his own excellence, and wishing to make himself his own end, not according to naked and simple faith, but according to natural conditions, which carried him on to an extravagant and disordered love of himself. This is the lie in which live all those who do not adhere with simplicity and nakedness of faith to the word of God, but wish to live according to human prudence, which is nothing more than an ants' nest of lies and vain arguments. . . .

Francis

[26] John 8:44.

6

"There are two principal reasons for prayer"

*To a young woman
having difficulty praying*

Mademoiselle,

Some time ago I received one of your letters, which I greatly value, because it testifies to the confidence you have in my love, which indeed is really yours; do not doubt it. I only regret that I am hardly capable of answering what you ask me concerning your troubles in prayer. I know that you are in a place and in a company in which you cannot lack good advice about this problem, but charity, which loves to communicate itself, makes you ask mine in giving me yours. I will therefore say something to you.

The disquietude you have in prayer, which is joined with a very eager anxiety to find some object that may content your spirit, is enough in itself to hinder you from getting what you seek. When we seek a thing with too much excitement, we pass our hand and our eyes over it a hundred times without noticing it at all.

Thy Will Be Done

From this vain and useless eagerness you can only incur lassitude of spirit; and from this comes the coldness and numbness of your soul. I know not the remedies you should use, but I feel sure that if you can prevent this eagerness you will gain much, for it is one of the greatest traitors that devotion and true virtue can meet with. It pretends to excite us to good, but only to make us tepid; it only makes us run in order to make us stumble. This is why we must always beware of it, and especially in prayer.

To aid yourself in this, remember that the graces and goods of prayer are not waters of earth but of Heaven, and that our own efforts will never be sufficient to obtain them. Of course, we must dispose ourselves for them with a great care, but with a humble and quiet care. We must keep our hearts open to Heaven, and wait for the holy dew. And we must never forget to carry with us into prayer the knowledge that in it we approach God and place ourselves in His presence for two principal reasons.

First, we pray in order to give God the honor and homage we owe Him; and this can be done without His speaking to us or we to Him, for this duty is paid by remembering that He is our God and we are His vile creatures, and by remaining prostrate in spirit before Him, awaiting His commands.

How many courtiers go a hundred times into the presence of the king, not to hear him or speak to him, but simply to be seen by him, and to testify by this assiduity that they are his servants? And this purpose in prostrating ourselves before God — to testify to and profess our good will and gratitude in His service — is excellent, holy, and pure, and therefore of the greatest perfection.

Second, we pray in order to speak with God, and to hear Him speak to us by inspirations and movements in the interior of our soul. And generally this is with a very delicious pleasure, because it is a great good for us to speak to so great a Lord; and when He answers, He spreads abroad a thousand precious balms and unguents, which give great sweetness to the soul.

Well, my good daughter, one of these two goods can never fail you in prayer. If we can speak to our Lord, let us speak, let us praise Him, beseech Him, listen to Him. If we cannot use our voice, still let us stay in the room and do reverence to Him. He will see us there; He will accept our patience, and will favor our silence. Another time we shall be quite amazed to be taken by the hand and He will converse with us, and will make a hundred turns with us in the walks of His garden of prayer. And if He should never do this, let us be content with our duty of being in His suite, and with the great grace and too great honor He does us in suffering our presence.

Thus we shall not be overeager to speak to Him, since it is no less useful for us just to be in His presence; yea, it is more useful, although not so much to our taste. When, then, you come to Him, speak to Him if you can. If you cannot, stay there; be seen; and care for nothing else.

Such is my advice. I do not know if it is good, but I am not too much concerned about it, because, as I have said, you are where much better advice cannot fail you.

As to your fear that your father may make you lose your desire to be a Carmelite by the long time he requires you to wait, say to God, "Lord, all my desire is before you,"[27] and let

---

[27] Ps. 37:10 (RSV = Ps. 38:9).

Thy Will Be Done

Him act; He will turn your father's heart and arrange for His own glory and your good. Meanwhile nourish your good desire, and keep it alive under the ashes of humility and resignation to the will of God.

My prayers, which you ask, are not wanting to you. For I could not forget you, especially at holy Mass; I trust to your charity not to be forgotten in yours. . . .

Francis

7

"Little virtues prepare for contemplation of God"

*To Jane de Chantal,
on prayer and virtue*

My dear child,

Each one must love the virtues that are suitable to him, each according to his vocation. The virtues of a widow are humility, contempt of the world and of oneself, and simplicity. Her exercises are love of her abjection, the service of the poor and ill; her place, the foot of the Cross; her rank, the last; her glory, to be scorned; her crown must be her misery: these are small virtues. Regarding ecstasies, insensibilities, deifying unions, elevations, transformations, and states in which one deems it a distraction to serve our Savior in His humanity and in His members (and in which one no longer takes any amusement except in the contemplation of the divine essence), we must leave these for the rare souls who are elevated and worthy of them. We do not merit such a rank in the service of God; one must serve Him first in lowly offices, before being appointed to His cabinet.

Thy Will Be Done

See your Abbess[28] in every place that she is. See her in her chamber in Nazareth: she exercises her modesty in being fearful, her candor in desiring to be informed and questioning, her resignation and humility in calling herself a handmaid. See her in Bethlehem: she lives a simple life of poverty; she listens to the shepherds as if they were great doctors. Look at her with the kings: never does she take it upon herself to harangue them. See her in the Purification: she goes to obey the ecclesiastical custom. In going to and returning from Egypt, she simply obeys St. Joseph. In visiting her holy cousin Elizabeth out of a charitable graciousness, she does not believe that she wastes time. She looks for our Lord not in rejoicing, but in crying. She has compassion for the poverty and embarrassment of those who invited her to the wedding at Cana, obtaining for them their necessities. She is at the foot of the Cross humbly, lowly, and virtuously.

God does not reward His servants according to the dignity of the office they exercise. I do not say that one should not aspire to these high and supreme virtues, but I say that one must exercise oneself in the little ones, without which the great ones are often false and deceitful. Let us learn to suffer voluntarily words of abasement and words that serve to snub our opinions and our views; then we will learn to suffer martyrdom, annihilation in God, and insensibility in all things. David learned first to butcher animals and then to destroy armies.[29] One knows what Eliezer did to learn if Rebecca was suitable to be the spouse of the son of his master Abraham. He

---

[28] Our Lady.

[29] 1 Kings 17:34-37 (RSV = 1 Sam. 17:34-37).

asked her for a drink of water: she proved her suitability when she willingly gave it to him and proved it again when she willingly gave it to his camels.[30] A little courtesy, a small virtue — but the mark of a true greatness.

I do not forbid elevation of the soul, mental prayer, interior conversation with God, and the perpetual transport of the heart in our Savior; but do you know what I want to say, my daughter? You must be like the "strong woman"[31] of whom the sage says, "She has put out her hand to strong things, and her fingers have taken hold of the spindle."[32] Meditate, lift your spirit, bear it in God — that is, bear God in your spirit: here are the "strong things." But with all of this, do not forget your distaff and your spindle: thread the string of little virtues, lower yourself to exercises of charity. He who says otherwise is mistaken. . . .

Always make your way before God and before yourself. God takes pleasure to see you take your little steps; and like a good father who holds his child by the hand, He will accommodate His steps to yours and will be content to go no faster than you. Why do you worry? . . .

Walk joyously, my daughter, with a tremendous confidence in the mercy of your Spouse, and believe that He will lead you well; but let Him do it.

Francis

---

[30] Gen. 24:13-20.
[31] Prov. 31:10.
[32] Ibid., 31:19.

8

"We must remain in the presence of God"

To Jane de Chantal, on prayer

My dearest child,

Your manner of prayer is good, but be very careful to remain near God in this gentle and quiet attention of heart, and in this sweet slumber in the arms of His holy will, for all this is agreeable to Him.

In praying this way, avoid strenuous efforts to understand, because they hurt you, not only in other matters, but even in prayer; circle around the dear object of your meditation with your affections quite simply, and as gently as you can. Your understanding will surely make some dartings to intrude itself, but you must not busy yourself to keep on your guard against it, for that would form a distraction. But when you perceive it, be satisfied with returning to the simple act of the will.

To *keep* ourselves in the presence of God and to *place* ourselves in the presence of God are, in my opinion, two different things. For to place ourselves in this presence it is necessary to recall our minds from every other object and render it actually attentive to the divine presence, as I say in my book.[33]

But after placing ourselves in the presence of God, we keep ourselves there by making certain acts toward God, either by understanding or by will. We can make these acts by looking at Him or by looking at some other thing for love of Him. We can make them by looking at nothing, and instead by speaking to Him. Lastly, we can make them by neither looking nor speaking, but simply by staying where He has put us, like a statue in its niche.

When there is added to this simple *staying* some feeling that we belong completely to God, and that He is our all, we must indeed give thanks to His goodness. If a statue that had been placed in a niche in some room could speak and was asked, "Why are you there?" it would say, "Because my master has put me here."

"Why don't you move?"

"Because he wants me to remain immovable."

"What use are you there; what do you gain by being so?"

"It is not for my profit that I am here; it is to serve and obey the will of my master."

"But you do not see him."

"No, but he sees me, and takes pleasure in seeing me where he has put me."

"Would you not like to have movement, so that you could go nearer to him?"

"Certainly not, except when he might command me."

"Don't you want anything, then?"

---

[33] *Introduction to the Devout Life,* Part 2, ch. 2.

"No; for I am where my master has placed me, and his good pleasure is the unique contentment of my being."

My God! What a good prayer and a good way to keep in the presence of God, to keep ourselves in His will and His good pleasure! I think that Magdalen was a statue in her niche, when without speaking, without moving, and perhaps without looking at Him, she listened to what our Lord said, seated at His feet.[34] When He spoke she heard; when He paused from speaking, she ceased to listen, and still stayed *ever there*.

A little child who is on the bosom of its sleeping mother is truly in its good and desirable place, although it says no word to her nor she to it.

My God! How glad I am, my child, to speak a little of these things with you! How happy we are when we will to love our Lord! Let us, then, love Him well. Let us not set ourselves to consider too exactly what we do for His love, provided we know that we will to do nothing but for His love.

For my part, I think we keep ourselves in the presence of God even while sleeping. For we go to sleep in His sight, by His will, and at His pleasure; and He puts us there like statues in a niche. And when we wake we find that He is there near us; He has not moved any more than we; we have then kept in His presence, but with our eyes shut and closed. . . .

Be resolute, dear child; doubt not. God holds you with His hand, and will never leave you. Glory be to Him for ever and ever! Amen.

Francis

[34] Luke 10:39.

9

"Never does God leave us save to hold us better"

*To Jane de Chantal,
in praise of the "little virtues"*

Dear child,

My God! When will the time come that our Lady will be born in our hearts?

For my part, I see that I am totally unworthy of it; you will think just the same of yourself. But her Son was born in the stable; so courage then; let us get a place prepared for this holy infant. Our Lady loves only places made low by humility, common by simplicity, but large by charity; she is willingly near the crib, and at the foot of the Cross; she does not mind if she goes into Egypt, far from all comfort, provided she has her dear Son with her.

No, our Lord may wrestle with us and throw us to left or to right; He may (as with other Jacobs) press us, may give to us a hundred twists, may engage us first on one side, and then on the other; in short, He may do us a thousand hurts. All the same, we will not leave Him until He gives us His eternal benediction.[35] And, my child, never does our good God leave us save to hold us better; never does He let go of us save to keep us better; never does He wrestle with us save to give Himself up to us and to bless us.

Let us advance, meanwhile, let us advance; let us make our way through these low valleys of the humble and little virtues. We shall see in them the roses amid the thorns, charity that shows its beauty among interior and exterior afflictions, the lilies of purity, the violets of mortification: what virtues shall we not see?

Above all, I love the three little virtues — sweetness of heart, poverty of spirit, and simplicity of life — and the substantial exercises — visiting the sick, serving the poor, comforting the afflicted, and the like. But the whole without eagerness, with a true liberty.

No, our arms are not yet long enough to reach the cedars of Lebanon; let us content ourselves with the hyssop of the valleys.

Francis

[35] Gen. 32.

Loving and Serving God in Your Daily Life

10

"Marriage is an exercise in mortification"

*To a young woman
contemplating marriage*

Mademoiselle,

I answer your letter of the second of this month, later than I wished, considering the quality of the advice and counsel you ask me; but the great rains have hindered travellers from starting. At least I have had no safe opportunity until this.

The advice your good cousin so constantly gave you to remain your own mistress, in the care of your father, and able afterward to consecrate your heart and body to our Lord, was founded on a great number of considerations drawn from many circumstances relating to your condition. For this reason, if your spirit had been in a full and entire indifference, I should doubtless have told you that you should follow that advice as the noblest and most proper that could be offered, for it would have been such beyond all question.

But since your spirit is not at all indifferent, but rather quite bent to the choice of marriage, and since in spite of your recourse to God you feel yourself still attached to marriage, it is not expedient to do violence to so confirmed a feeling for any reason whatever. All the circumstances that otherwise would be more than enough to make me agree with your dear cousin, have no weight against this strong inclination and propensity, which, indeed, if it were weak and slight, would be of little account, but being powerful and firm, must be the foundation of your resolution.

If then the husband proposed to you is otherwise suitable — a good man, and of sympathetic humor — you may profitably accept him. I say sympathetic, because this bodily defect of yours[36] requires sympathy, as it requires you to compensate for it by a great sweetness, a sincere love, and a very resigned humility — in short, true virtue and perfection of soul must cover over the deficiency of body. . . .

The state of marriage is one that requires more virtue and constancy than any other. It is a perpetual exercise of mortification; it will perhaps be so to you more than usual. You must then dispose yourself to it with a particular care, that from this thyme plant, in spite of the bitter nature of its juice, you may be able to draw and make the honey of a holy life.

May the sweet Jesus be ever your sugar and your honey to sweeten your vocation; ever may He live and reign in our hearts. I am in Him,

Your very affectionate servant,

Francis

---

[36] Extremely short stature.

11

"As far as possible, make your devotion attractive"

*To a married woman, on
harmonizing family and devotion*

Madame,

I cannot give you all at once what I promised, because I do not
have sufficient time to put together all that I have to tell you
on the subject you want me to explain. I will therefore tell it
to you in several letters. Besides the convenience to me, you
will have the advantage of having time to ruminate on my
advice properly.

You have a great desire for Christian perfection. It is the
most generous desire you could have: feed it and make it grow
every day. The means of gaining perfection are various according to the variety of vocations: religious, widows, and married
persons must all seek after this perfection, but not all by the
same means.

For you, Madame, who are married, the means of gaining
perfection are to unite yourself closely to God and to your
neighbor, and to what belongs to them. The means to unite

yourself to God are, chiefly, the use of the sacraments and prayer. As to the use of the sacraments, you should let no month go without receiving Communion. After some time, and under the advice of your spiritual fathers, you will be able to receive Communion more often.

As to confession, I advise you to frequent it even more, especially if you fall into some imperfection by which your conscience is troubled, as often happens at the beginning of the spiritual life. Still, if you have not the opportunity for confession, contrition and repentance will do.

As to prayer, you should apply yourself to it much, and especially to meditation, for which you are, I think, well suited. Make, then, a short hour every day in the morning before going out, or else before the evening meal; and be very careful not to make it either after dinner or after supper, for that would hurt your health.

And to help yourself to do it well, you must previously know the point on which you are to meditate, so that in beginning your prayer you may have your matter ready. For this purpose you may use books by the authors who have treated the points of meditation on the life and death of our Lord, such as Granada,[37] Bellintani, Capiglia,[38] and Bruno. Choose the meditation you wish to make and read it attentively, so as to remember it at the time of prayer, and not to have anything more to do except to recall the points, always following the method that I gave you on Holy Thursday.

---

[37] *The Memorial of the Christian Life*, 1565, 1574.

[38] André Capiglia (died 1610), Spanish Carthusian, author of a book of *Meditations on the Gospels*.

Make your devotion attractive

Besides this, often make spontaneous prayers to our Lord, at every moment you can, and in all companies, always seeing God in your heart and your heart in God.

Take pleasure in reading Granada's books on prayer and meditation,[39] for none teach you better, nor with more stirring power. I should like you to let no day pass without giving half an hour to the reading of some spiritual book, for this would serve as a sermon.

These are the chief means to unite yourself closely to God. Those to unite yourself properly with your neighbor are in great number; but I will only mention some of them.

We must regard our neighbor in God, who wills that we should love and cherish him. It is the counsel of St. Paul, who orders servants to serve God in their masters and to serve their masters in God.[40] We must exercise ourselves in this love of our neighbor, expressing it externally. And although it may seem at first against our will, we must not give up on that account; our repugnance will at last be conquered by habit and good inclination, which will be produced by repetition of the acts. We must refer our prayers and meditations to this end: for after having prayed to love God, we must always pray to love our neighbor, and especially those to whom our will is not attracted.

I advise you to take care sometimes to visit hospitals, comfort the sick, pity their infirmities, soften your heart toward them, and pray for them, at the same time giving them some help.

---

[39] Louis de Granada, *On Prayer and Discernment*, 1554.
[40] Eph. 6:5-7.

Thy Will Be Done

But in all this take particular care that your husband, your servants, and your parents do not suffer by your too long stayings in church, by your too great retirement, or by your failing to care for your household. And do not become, as often happens, manager of others' affairs, or too contemptuous of conversations in which the rules of devotion are not quite exactly observed. In all this charity must rule and enlighten us, to make us condescend to the wishes of our neighbor in what is not against the commandments of God.

You must not only be devout, and love devotion, but you must make it lovable to everyone. Well, you will render it lovable if you render it useful and agreeable. The sick will love your devotion if they are charitably consoled by it; your family will love it if they find you more careful of their welfare, more gentle in little accidents that happen, more kind in correcting, and so on; your husband, if he sees that as your devotion increases you are more devoted in his regard, and sweet in your love to him; your parents and friends if they perceive in you more generosity, tolerance, and condescension toward their wills, when not against the will of God. In short, you must, as far as possible, make your devotion attractive. . . .

I beg you to give me some part in your prayers and Communions, as I assure you I will give you, all my life, a share in mine, and will be without end, Madame,

Your most affectionate servant in Jesus Christ,

Francis

12

"Have patience with everyone, including yourself"

———

To a woman beset by many tasks

My dear daughter,

I remember you telling me how much the multiplicity of your affairs weighs on you; and I said to you that it is a good opportunity for acquiring the true and solid virtues. The multiplicity of affairs is a continual martyrdom, for just as flies cause more pain and irritation to those who travel in summer than the travelling itself does, just so the diversity and the multitude of affairs causes more pain than the weight of these affairs itself.

You need patience, and I hope that God will give it to you (if you ask it of Him carefully) and that you will try to practice it faithfully, preparing yourself for it every morning by a special application of some point in your meditation, and resolving to restore yourself to patience throughout the day as many times as you sense yourself becoming distracted.

Do not lose any occasion, however small it may be, for exercising gentleness of heart toward everyone. Do not think that you will be able to succeed in your affairs by your own efforts, but only by the assistance of God; and on setting out, consign yourself to His care, believing that He will do that which will be best for you, provided that, on your part, you employ a gentle diligence. I say "gentle diligence," because violent diligence spoils the heart and affairs, and is not diligence, but haste and trouble.

My God, Madame, we will soon be in eternity, and then we will see how all the affairs of this world are such little things and how little it matters whether they turn out or not. At this time, nevertheless, we apply ourselves to them as if they were great things. When we were little children, with what eagerness did we put together little bits of tile, wood, and mud, to make houses and small buildings! And if someone destroyed them, we were very grieved and tearful at it; but now we know well that it all mattered very little. One day it will be the same with us in Heaven, when we will see that our concerns in this world were truly only child's play.

I do not want to take away the care that we must have regarding these little trifles, because God has entrusted them to us in this world for exercise; but I would indeed like to take away the passion and anxiety of this care. Let us do our child's play, because we are children; but also, let us not trouble ourselves to death in playing it. And if someone destroys our little houses and little designs, let us not torment ourselves greatly at this; because also, when this night comes in which it will be necessary for us to take shelter — I mean to say, death — all these little houses will be of no use to us; we will have to take our shelter in the house of our Father. Faithfully attend to your obligations, but know that you have no greater obligation than that of your salvation and of the saving progress of your soul on the way to true devotion.

Have patience with everyone, but chiefly with yourself; I mean to say, do not trouble yourself about your imperfections, and always have the courage to lift yourself out of them. I am well content that you begin again every day: there is no better way to perfect the spiritual life than always to begin again and never to think you have done enough.

Recommend me to the mercy of God, which I ask to make you abound in His holy love. Amen. I am

Your most humble servant,

Francis

13.

"Keep yourself gentle amid household troubles"

To a busy housewife,
on maintaining spiritual calm

My dearest daughter,

Whenever I can manage it, you shall have a letter from me. But at present I write to you the more readily, because Monsieur Moyron, my present bearer, is my nearest neighbor in this town, my great friend and ally, by whom, on his return, you will be able to write to me in all confidence, and if the picture of St. Teresa of Avila is finished, he will take it, pay for it, and bring it, as I have asked him to do.

But, my daughter, I suspect that I did not tell you exactly, in my last letter, what I wanted to say concerning your little but frequent impatiences in the accidents of your housekeeping. I tell you, then, that you must pay special attention to this, and that you must keep yourself gentle in them, and that when you get up in the morning, or leave prayer, or return from Mass or Communion, and always when you return to domestic affairs, you must be attentive to beginning quietly. Every now

51

and then you must look at your heart to see if it is in a state of gentleness. If it is not gentle, make it so before all things; and if it is gentle, you must praise God, and use this gentleness in the affairs that present themselves with a special care not to let it get disturbed.

You see, my daughter, those who often eat honey find bitter things more bitter and sour things more sour, and are easily disgusted with coarse meats. Your soul, often occupying itself with spiritual exercises that are sweet and agreeable to the spirit, when it returns to corporal matters, exterior and material, finds them very rough and disagreeable, and so it easily gets impatient. And therefore, my dear daughter, you must see in these exercises the will of God, which is there, and not merely the thing that is done.

Often invoke the unique and lovely Dove of the celestial Spouse, that He would entreat for you a true dove's heart, and that you may be a dove, not only when flying in prayer, but also inside your nest and with all those who are around you. God be forever in the midst of your heart, my dear child, and make you one spirit with Him!

I salute through you the good mother Louise of Jesus and all the Carmelite sisters, imploring the aid of their prayers. If I knew that our dear Sister Jacob were there, I would salute her also, and her little Françon; as I do your Madeleine, who is also mine. *Vive Jésus!*[41]

Francis

---

[41] "Live Jesus!"

14.

"Do what you see can be done with love"

To a wife having difficulties
living with her parents-in-law

My dearest child,

Once more, my very dear daughter, I have no leisure in which to write to you, although I answer your letter tardily.

Well, now, here you are in your establishment, and you cannot alter it; you must be what you are, mother of a family, since you have a husband and children. And you must be so with good heart, and with love of God, yea, *for* the love of God (as I say clearly enough to Philothea[42]), without troubling or disquieting yourself any more than you can help.

But I see well, my dearest daughter, that it is a little uncomfortable for you to have charge of the housekeeping in a home where there is a father and mother. For I have never seen that fathers — and still less mothers — leave the entire

---

[42] *Introduction to the Devout Life,* Part 3, ch. 38. Philothea ("Lover of God") is the fictional addressee of the advice in the *Introduction.*

management of the house to the daughters, although sometimes they should. For my part, I counsel you to do as gently and nicely as you can that which is recommended, never breaking peace with your father and mother. It is better that the running of the household be not exactly as you would wish, if this will please those to whom you owe so much.

And then, unless I deceive myself, your character is not made for fighting. Peace is better than a fortune. You must do what you see can be done with love; in the case of persons so greatly to be respected, you must not do what can only be accomplished with strife. I have no doubt there will be aversions and repugnances in your spirit. But, my dearest daughter, these are so many occasions to exercise the true virtue of sweetness; for we must do well and in a holy and loving way what we owe to every one, although it may be against the grain and without relish. . . .

Embrace holy prayer. Often throw your heart into the hands of God, rest your soul in His love, and put your cares under His protection, whether for the voyage of your dear husband or for your other affairs.

Do well what you can, and the rest leave to God, who will do it sooner or later, according to the disposition of His divine Providence. . . . To sum up, be ever all God's, my dearest daughter; and I am in Him

Your most humble cousin
and very affectionate servant,

Francis

15

"Parents can demand more than God Himself"

*To a widow, on her
duties to her mother*

Madame,

I should be quite troubled in writing to you on this present subject if I were not authorized by Madame, your mother. For on what ground could I intervene in what passes between you two, and how appeal to your conscience, knowing that you are the only and worthy daughter of a worthy mother, who is full of sense, prudence, and piety? However, since I must intervene, then, under this authorization, I will.

Your mother has written to me all that she has told you herself (and that she has had many excellent persons, in comparison with whom I am nothing, tell you) to bring you around to her desire that you not deprive her of your filial help in these great straits to which the occurrences you know of have reduced her. She cannot bear to see her estate collapse under the burden, and above all, for the want of your help, which she considers to be all that is necessary.

Thy Will Be Done

She proposes three plans: either that you enter a religious order, in order that the creditors may no longer want you as security, and that she may have the free disposal of your children's property; or that you marry again with the advantages that are offered you; or that you remain with her and keep a common purse.

She gives in her letter the exceptions you take to the first two plans. She says you have vowed your chastity to God, and that you have four very little children, of whom two are girls; but about the third plan I see nothing in her letter.

As to the first plan, I do not want to interpose my judgment on the question of whether your vow obliges you not to ask a dispensation (although she alleges a great hastiness that may have prevented due consideration). For indeed the purity of chastity is of such high price that whoever has vowed it is very happy to keep it, and there is nothing to prefer to it except the necessity of the public good.

As to the second plan, I do not know whether you can lawfully give up that care of your children that God has required from you in making you their mother, especially since they are so little.

But as to the third, Madame, I say that your purse ought to be common with your mother, in a case of such great necessity. Oh God! It is the least we owe to father and mother. I suspect that I can indeed discern some reason why a daughter, so placed with children, might keep her purse to herself. But I do not know whether reason to do so exists in your particular case; and if it does, it must be very clear and strong, and bear to be seen and examined thoroughly. Among enemies, extreme necessity makes all things common; but among friends, and such friends as daughters and mothers, we must not wait for extreme necessity, for the command of God urges us too much. In such cases we must lift up our eyes and heart to the Providence of God, who returns abundantly all that we give according to His holy commandment.

I say too much, Madame; for I had no right to speak on this, except to refer your dear conscience in this regard to those to whom you confide it. . . .

O my God! Dear lady, what we should do for fathers and mothers! And how lovingly must we support the excess, the zeal, and the ardor — I had almost said "the importunity" — of their love! These mothers — they are altogether wonderful; they would like, I think, always to carry their children, particularly an only child, at their breasts. They often feel jealous if their child takes a little amusement out of their presence; they consider that they are never loved enough, and that the love that is due to them can never be fully measured except when it is beyond proper measure.

How can we mend this? We must have patience, and do, as nearly as we can, all that is required to correspond with it. God requires of us only certain days, certain hours, and His presence is quite content that we also be present with fathers and mothers; but these latter are more exacting. They require many more days and hours, and an undivided presence. Ah! God is so good that, condescending to this, He reckons the accommodation of our will to our mother's as accommodation to His, provided His good pleasure is the principal end of our actions.

Well, then, you have Moses and the prophets — that is, so many excellent servants of God: hear them. And as for me, I

Thy Will Be Done

do wrong to occupy you so long, but I have a little pleasure in speaking with a pure and chaste soul, and one against which there is no complaint, except for excess of devotion — a rare complaint, so rare and admirable that I cannot help loving and honoring her who is accused of it, or being for ever, Madame,

Your very humble and obedient servant,

Francis

16

"Avoid making your devotion troublesome"

To a married woman, whose
relatives interfere with her devotions

Madame my sister,

I wrote to you six weeks ago to answer all you asked me, and have no doubt you got my letter, which will make me more brief in this one. . . .

Regarding our little sister, I leave her to you, and put myself in no trouble about her. Only I should not like your father to fear she might become too devout, as he has always had fear of you; for I am certain she will not sin by excess on that side. My God! The good father we have, and the good husband you have! They are a little jealous for their empire and dominion, which seems to them somewhat violated when anything is done without their authority and command. What can be done? We must allow them this little bit of human nature.

They want to be masters, and is that not right? Truly it is, regarding the duties that you owe them. But these good men do not realize that in regard to the good of the soul you must trust spiritual doctors and directors, and that (except where your father and husband have authority over you) you must obtain your interior good by the means judged fitting by those appointed to conduct souls.

But still, regarding your father and husband, you must condescend greatly to their will, bear with their little fancies, and bend as much as you can without spoiling our good designs. These condescensions will please our Lord. I have told you before: the less we live after our own taste, and the less of choice there is in our actions, the more of solidity and goodness there is in our devotion. We must sometimes leave our Lord in order to please others for the love of Him.

No, I cannot refrain, my dear child, from telling you my thought. I know that you will take my advice in a good way, because I speak with sincerity. Perhaps you have given occasion to your good father and good husband to mix themselves up with your devotion, and to be restive about it; I cannot tell how. Perhaps you are a little too eager and bustling, and you have wanted to bother and restrict them. If so, that is without doubt the cause that makes them now withdraw. We must, if possible, avoid making our devotion troublesome.

Now, I tell you what you must do. When you can receive Communion without troubling your two superiors, do so, according to the advice of your confessor. When you are afraid that it will trouble them, receive Communion in spirit; and believe me this spiritual mortification, this privation of God, will please God extremely, and will advance your heart greatly. We must sometimes take a step back to get a better spring.

I have often admired the extreme resignation of St. John the Baptist, who remained so long in the desert, quite close to our Lord, without hastening to see Him, to hear Him, and to follow Him. And I have wondered how, after having seen and baptized Him, he could let Jesus go without attaching himself to Him in body, as he was so closely united to Him in heart. But he knew that he served this same Lord by this privation of His real presence.

So I say that God will be served if, for a little, to gain the heart of the two superiors whom He has appointed, you suffer the loss of His real Communion; and it will be to me a great consolation, if I know that these counsels that I give you do not disquiet your heart. Believe me, this resignation, this abnegation will be very useful to you.

You may, however, take advantage of secret opportunities of Communion. For provided that you can defer and accommodate yourself to the will of these two persons, and do not make them impatient, I give you no other rule for your Communions than that which your confessors may give you; for they see the present state of your interior, and can understand what is required for your good. . . .

You are, as far as I see, in the true way to resignation and indifference, since you cannot serve God at your will. I know a lady, one of the greatest souls I have ever met, who has long remained in such subjection to the humors of her husband, that in the very height of her devotions and ardors, she was obliged to wear a low dress, and was all loaded with vanity outside, and except at Easter could never receive Communion unless secretly and unknown to every one; otherwise she would have excited a thousand storms in her house. And by this road she rose very high, as I know, having been her father confessor very often.

Thy Will Be Done

Mortify yourself, then, joyously; and in proportion as you are hindered from doing the good you desire, do the good that you do not desire. You do not desire these resignations; you would desire others. But do those that you do not desire, for they are worth more. . . .

Keep your heart very wide to receive in it all sorts of crosses and resignations or abnegations, for the love of Him who has received so many of them for us. May His name be forever blessed and His kingdom be confirmed forever and ever! I am in Him, and by Him,

Your, and more than your, brother and servant,

Francis

17

"Have contempt for contempt"

---

*To a woman angered
by her broken engagement*

Mademoiselle,

Regarding the first part of the letter you wrote to Madame N. and which you wished to be communicated to me, my dearest daughter, I will say that if Monsieur N. made to you no other assertions than those you give, and if the matter were before us, we would require him to marry you, under heavy penalties. For he has no right, on account of considerations that he could and should have made before his promise, to break his word. But I do not know how things go over in the place in which you live, where often the rules that we have in our ecclesiastical affairs are not known.

Meantime, my dearest daughter, my desire to dissuade you from prosecuting this wretched lawsuit did not arise from doubt about your rights, but from the aversion and bad opinion I have of all legal battles. Truly the result of a lawsuit must be marvelously happy, to compensate for the expense, the bitterness, the anxious excitements, the dissipation of heart, the atmosphere of reproaches, and the multitude of inconveniences that prosecutions usually bring. Above all I consider worrying and useless — yea, injurious — the suits that arise from injurious words and breaches of promise when there is no real interest at stake. This is because instead of eradicating insults, lawsuits publish, increase, and continue them; and instead of causing the fulfilment of promises, lawsuits drive the other party to the other extreme.

Look, my dear daughter, I consider that in truth, contempt for contempt is the testimony of generosity that we give by our disdain for the weakness and inconstancy of those who break faith with us; it is the best remedy of all. Most injuries are more happily met by the contempt that is shown for them than by any other means; the blame remains rather with the injurer than with the injured. . . .

I will then pray our Lord to give you a good and holy result to this affair, that you may attain a solid and constant tranquillity of heart, which can only be obtained in God, in whose holy love I wish that you may more and more progress. God bless you with His great blessings. That is, my dear child, may God make you perfectly His. I am in Him

Your very affectionate and humble servant,

Francis

18

"Lord, what would You have me do?"

---

*To a man wondering if
he has a religious vocation*

Sir,

Go and bless our Lord for the favorable inspiration He has given you to withdraw yourself from this great and wide road that those of your age and profession are accustomed to follow, and by which they ordinarily arrive at a thousand kinds of vices and inconveniences, and very often at eternal damnation. Meanwhile, to make this divine vocation fruitful, to realize more clearly the state that you are about to choose, and to better satisfy this infinite mercy, which invites you to His perfect love, I counsel you to practice these exercises for the following three months.

First, refrain from some satisfactions of the senses, which you might take without offending God. For this purpose, always rise at six, whether you have slept well or badly, provided you are not ill (for in that case you would have to condescend to the sickness); and to do something more on

Fridays, rise at five. This arrangement will give you more leisure to make your prayer and reading.

Also, accustom yourself to say every day, after or before prayer, fifteen Our Fathers, and fifteen Hail Marys, with your arms extended in the form of a cross.

Moreover, renounce the pleasures of taste, eating those meats at table that may be less agreeable to you, provided they are not unwholesome, and leaving those to which your taste may have more inclination. . . .

These little light austerities will serve you to a double end: the one, to entreat more surely the light required for your spirit to make its choice (for the lowering of the body in those who have entire strength and health marvelously raises the spirit); the other, to try and to feel austerity, in order to see if you could embrace it, and what repugnance you will have to it. This experiment is necessary to test the slight inclination you have to leave the world. If you are faithful in the practice of the little things that I propose to you, you will be able to judge what you would be in those greater things that are practiced in religious orders.

Pray earnestly to our Lord to illuminate you, and say often to Him the words of St. Paul, "Lord, what would you have me to do?"[43] and those of David, "Teach me to do Thy will, for Thou art my God."[44] Above all, if you awaken during the night, employ well this time in speaking to our Lord about your choice. Protest often to His majesty that you resign to Him and leave in His hands the disposition of all the moments

---

[43] Acts 9:6.
[44] Ps. 142:10 (RSV = Ps. 143:10).

of your life, and that He must please dispose of them according to His will.

Fail not to make your prayers morning and evening, when you can, with a little retreat before supper, to lift up your heart unto our Lord.

Take up pastimes that are of the more vigorous kind, such as riding, leaping, and the like; and not the soft ones, such as cards and dancing. But if you are touched with some vainglory about those others — "Alas!" you must say, "what does all this profit one for eternity?"

Go to Communion every Sunday, and always with prayers beg the light you need; and on feast days you may well visit, as an exercise, holy places — the Capuchins, St. Bernard's, the Carthusians.

If you feel the inspiration toward religion gather strength and your heart urged by it, take counsel with your confessor; and in case you make a resolution, gradually dispose your grandfather toward it, so that the annoyance and pain caused by your leaving may fall as little as possible on religion, and that you only may be burdened with it.

May God grant you His peace, His grace, His light, and His most holy consolation.

Francis

19

"Take Jesus as your patron"

---

*To a young man
going to live at court*

Sir,

At last, then, you are going to make sail, and take the open sea of the world at court! God be gracious to you, and may His holy hand be ever with you!

I am not so fearful as many others, and I do not think that this is one of the most dangerous professions for those of noble soul and manly heart. For there are but two principal rocks in this gulf: vanity, which ruins spirits that are soft, slothful, feminine, and weak; and ambition, which ruins audacious and presumptuous hearts.

Vanity is a *defect* of courage, and lacks the strength to undertake the acquisition of true and solid praise, but desires and is content with the false and the empty. Just so, ambition is an *excess* of courage, which leads us to pursue glories and honors without and against the rule of reason.

Thus vanity causes us to occupy ourselves with those silly gallantries that are fashionable with women and other little spirits, but scorned by great hearts and elevated souls. And ambition makes us desire honors before deserving them. It is ambition that makes us put to our own credit, and at too high price, the merit of our predecessors; and we would willingly gain our esteem from theirs.

Well, sir, against all this, since it pleases you that I speak so, continue to nourish your soul with spiritual and divine meats, for they will make us strong against vanity and just against ambition.

Keep carefully to frequent Communion: believe me, you could do nothing more certain to strengthen yourself in virtue. To make yourself quite safe in this practice, put yourself under the orders of some good confessor, and beseech him to charge himself with making you give an account in confession of the failures you may make in this exercise, if by chance you make any. Always confess humbly, and with a true and express purpose of amendment.

I solemnly implore you: before leaving your home in the morning, never forget to ask on your knees for the help of our Lord; and before going to bed at night, never forget to ask for the pardon of your sins.

Especially beware of bad books; and for nothing in the world let your soul be carried away by certain writings that weak brains admire, because of some vain subtleties that they find in them. Such are the works of that infamous Rabelais,[45] and certain others of our age, who profess to doubt everything, to despise everything, and to scoff at all the maxims of antiquity. On the contrary, read books of solid doctrine

---

[45] François Rabelais (1494-1553), French author.

— and especially Christian and spiritual ones — for recreation from time to time.

I recommend to you that gentle and sincere courtesy which offends no one and obliges all, which seeks love rather than honor, which never rails at any one so as to hurt them, nor stingingly, which puts no one off and is itself never put off (or, if it is put off, it is but rarely, in exchange for which it is very often honorably advanced).

Take care, I beseech you, not to embarrass yourself in flirtations, and not to allow your affections to prevent your judgment and reason in the choice of objects of love; for when once inclination has taken its course, it drags the judgment like a slave to decisions that are very improper and are well worthy of the repentance that soon follows them.

I would wish that, first, in speech, in bearing, and in relations with others, you should make open and express profession of wishing to live virtuously, judiciously, perseveringly, and as a Christian.

I say "virtuously," that no one may attempt to engage you in immoralities. "Judiciously," that you may not show extreme signs, exteriorly, of your intention, but only such as, according to your condition, may not be censured by the wise.

"Perseveringly," because unless you show with perseverance an equal and inviolable will, you will expose your resolutions to the designs and attempts of many miserable souls, who attack others to draw them to their company.

Lastly, I say "as a Christian," because some make profession of wishing to be virtuous philosophically, who, however, are not so, and can in no way be so, and who are nothing else but phantoms of virtue, using their graceful manners and words to hide their bad life and ways from those who are not familiar with them.

But we — who well know that we cannot have a single particle of virtue but by the grace of our Lord — we must employ piety and holy devotion to live virtuously; otherwise we shall have virtues only in imagination and in shadow.

Now it is of the greatest importance to let ourselves be known right from the start such as we wish to be always, and in this we must have no haggling.

It is also of the greatest importance to make some friends who have the same aim, with whom you can associate and strengthen yourself. For it is a very true thing that the company of well-regulated souls is extremely useful to us to keep our own soul well regulated.

I think you will easily find either among the Jesuits, or the Capuchins, or the Feuillants, or even outside the monasteries, some gracious spirit who will be glad if you sometimes go to see him, for recreation, and to take spiritual breath.

But you must permit me to say to you one thing in particular. You see, sir, I fear you may return to gambling; and I fear this, because it will be to you a great evil: it would, in a few days, dissipate your heart, and make all the flowers of your good desires wither. Gambling is the occupation of an idler; and those who want to get renown and introductions by playing with the great, and who call this the best way of getting known, show that they have no good deserts, since they have no better credit than that of having money and wanting to risk it.

It is no great merit to be known as gamblers; but if they meet with great losses, every one knows them to be fools. I pass over the consequences, such as fights, despair, and madness, from which not one gambler has any exemption.

I wish you, further, a vigorous heart. Do not flatter your body by delicacies in eating, sleeping, and other such soft-nesses; for a generous heart has always a little contempt for bodily comforts and pleasures.

Still our Lord said that "those who are clothed in soft garments are in the houses of kings."[46] It is for this reason that I speak to you about it. Our Lord does not mean to say that all those who are in kings' houses must be clothed in soft gar-ments, but He says only that customarily those who clothe themselves softly are there. Of course, I am not speaking of the exterior of the clothing, but of the interior. For with regard to the exterior, you know far better what is proper; it is not for me to speak of it.

I mean, then, to say that I would like you sometimes to correct your body so far as to make it feel some rigors and hardships by contempt for delicacies and by frequent denial of things agreeable to the senses. Again, reason must sometimes exercise its superiority and the authority that it has to control the sensual appetites.

My God! I am too diffuse, and I scarcely know what I am saying, for it is without leisure and at odd moments. You know my heart, and will take all this well; but still I must say one thing more.

Imagine that you were a courtier of St. Louis. This holy king . . . loved for everyone to be brave, courageous, generous, good-humored, courteous, affable, free, and polite; and still he

---

[46] Matt. 11:8.

loved, above all, for everyone to be a good Christian. Had you been with him, you would have seen him kindly laughing on occasion, speaking boldly at the proper time, taking care that all was in splendor about him, like another Solomon, to maintain the royal dignity; and a moment afterward, he would be serving the poor in the hospitals, and marrying civil with Christian virtue and majesty with humility.

In a word, this is what we must seek: to be no less brave for being Christian, and no less Christian for being brave. For this we must be very good Christians — that is, very devout, pious, and if possible, spiritual. For, as St. Paul says, "the spiritual man discerneth all things":[47] he knows at what time, in what order, and by what method each virtue must be practiced.

Form often this good thought, that we are walking in this world between Paradise and Hell, and that our last step will place us in an eternal dwelling. We do not know which step will be our last, and so, in order to make our last step well, we must try to make all the others well.

O holy and unending eternity! Blessed is he who thinks of you. Yes, for what do we play here in this world but a children's game for who knows how many days? It would be nothing whatever, if it were not the passage to eternity.

On this account, therefore, we must pay attention to the time we have to dwell here below, and to all our occupations, so as to employ them in the conquest of the permanent good.

Love me always as yours, for I am so in our Lord, wishing you every happiness for this world and particularly for the other. May God bless you, and hold you by His holy hand.

---

[47] 1 Cor. 2:15.

Take Jesus as your patron

And to finish where I began: you are going to take the high sea of the world; change not, on that account, patron or sails, anchor or wind. Have Jesus always for your patron, His Cross for a mast on which you must spread your resolutions as a sail. Your anchor shall be a profound confidence in Him, and you shall sail prosperously.

May the favorable wind of celestial inspirations ever fill your vessel's sails fuller and fuller and make you happily arrive at the port of a holy eternity, which with true heart is wished you, sir, by

Your most humble servant,

Francis

20

"Remain innocent among the hissings of serpents"

---

*To a woman, on dealing
with improper conversations*

My dearest daughter,

Never think that geographical distance can ever separate souls whom God has united by the ties of His love. The children of the world are separated one from another because their hearts are in different places; but the children of God, having their hearts where their treasure is,[48] and sharing only one treasure — which is the same God — are consequently always united and joined together.

We must thus console our spirits in the necessity that keeps you away from this town, and which will soon force me to set out to return to my charge. We shall see one another very often again in prayer before our holy crucifix if we keep the promises we have made to one another; and it is there alone that our interviews are profitable.

[48] Cf. Luke 12:34.

Thy Will Be Done

Meanwhile, my dearest daughter, I will commence by telling you that you must fortify your spirit by all possible means against these vain apprehensions that generally agitate and torment you. And for this purpose regulate, in the first place, your spiritual exercises in such a way that their length may not weary your soul, nor trouble the souls of those with whom God makes you live. . . .

In a word, I wish you to be just Philothea, and no more than that: namely, what I describe in the book of the *Introduction to the Devout Life*,[49] which is written for you and for those in a similar state.

As to conversations, my dearest daughter, be at peace regarding what is said or done in them: for if they are good, you have something to praise God for, and if they are bad, you have something in which to serve God by turning your heart away from them. Do not appear either shocked or displeased by bad conversations, since you cannot prevent them, and have not authority enough to hinder the bad words of those who will say them, and who will say worse if you seem to wish to hinder them. For acting thus you will remain innocent among the hissings of the serpents, and like a sweet strawberry you will receive no venom from the contact of venomous tongues.

I cannot understand how you can admit these immoderate sadnesses into your heart. Being a child of God, long ago placed in the bosom of His mercy and consecrated to His love, you should comfort yourself, despising all these sad and melancholy suggestions. The enemy makes them to you, simply with the design of tiring and troubling you.

[49] *Introduction to the Devout Life*, Part 2, ch. 10.

Remain innocent among serpents

Take great pains to practice well the humble meekness that you owe to your dear husband and to everybody; for it is the virtue of virtues which our Lord has so much recommended to us. But if you happen to fail in it, do not distress yourself; simply with all confidence get up again on your feet to walk henceforward in peace and sweetness as before.

I send you a little method for uniting yourself to God, in the morning and all through the day. So much, my dear daughter, I have thought good to tell you for your comfort at present. It remains that I pray you not to make any ceremony with me, who have neither the leisure nor the will to make any with you. Write to me when you like, quite freely; for I shall always gladly receive news of your soul, which mine cherishes entirely, as in truth, my dearest daughter, I am

Your most humble servant in our Lord,

Francis

21

"Never speak evil of your neighbor"

To Jane de Chantal,
on not judging others

My dearest daughter,

I beg you never to speak evil of your neighbor or say anything, however little, which could offend him. Nevertheless, one must not approve of the evil, flatter it, or try to cover it up, but — when the welfare of the one of whom one speaks requires it — one must speak with candor and say frankly evil of evil, and blame blamable things; because in doing so, God is glorified. Above all, blame the vice and spare as much as possible the person to whom the vice belongs, all the more so because the goodness of God is so great that a single moment is sufficient for entreating His grace. And who can be sure that the one who yesterday was a sinner, and evil, will be so today?

When we look upon the actions of our neighbor, let us look on them in the light that is the gentlest; and when we can excuse neither the deed nor the intention of one whom we otherwise know to be good, let us not judge, but remove that

Thy Will Be Done

[impulse] from our spirit and leave the judgment to God. When we cannot excuse the sin, let us render it at least worthy of compassion, attributing it to the most tolerable cause, such as ignorance or infirmity. . . .

Francis

22

"Extravagant recreations may be blameworthy"

To a woman, on Christian entertainment

My dearest daughter,

You see what confidence I have in you. I have not written to you since your departure, because I really have not been able to do so; and I make you no excuse, because you are truly, and more and more, my more than most dear daughter.

God be praised that your journey back has been made quietly, and that you have found your husband happy. Truly, the heavenly Providence of the heavenly Father treats with sweetness the children of His heart, and from time to time mingles favorable sweetnesses with the fruitful bitternesses that merit such sweetnesses. . . .

Monsieur Michel asked me what I wrote to Monsieur Legrand about hunting; but, my dearest daughter, it was only a little thing in which I told him there were three laws to observe in order to avoid offending God in the chase.

First, we must not do damage to our neighbor, since it is not reasonable that any one should take his recreation at the expense of another, and especially in treading down the poor peasant, who is already martyred enough otherwise, and whose labor and condition we should not despise.

Second, we must not spend our time hunting on the days of the chief feasts in which we ought to serve God; and above all, we must take care not to omit Mass on the days we are commanded to attend it.

Finally, we must not spend too much money on hunting, for all recreations become blameworthy when extravagant.

I do not remember the rest [of what I said to Monsieur Legrand about hunting]. In general, discretion must reign everywhere.

So then, my dearest daughter, may God be ever in the midst of your heart, to unite all your affections to His holy love. Amen.

So has He, I assure you, put in my heart a most loving and complete affection for yours, which I cherish unceasingly, praying God to crown it with blessing.

Amen, my very dear, and ever more dear, daughter.

Francis

23

"We must not ask of ourselves what we don't have"

To a pregnant woman suffering lassitude and discouragement

My dearest daughter,

I am not at all surprised that your heart seems a little heavy and torpid, for you are pregnant, and it is an evident truth that our souls generally share in their inferior part the qualities and conditions of our bodies — and I say in the inferior part, my dearest daughter, because it is this that immediately touches the body, and which is liable to share in the troubles of it.

A delicate body that is weighed down by the burden of pregnancy, weakened by the labor of carrying a child, and troubled with many pains, does not allow the heart to be so lively, so active, so ready in its operations; but this in no way injures the acts of that higher part of the soul, which are as agreeable to God as they would be in the midst of all the gladnesses in the world. Yea, to God these acts are even more agreeable in truth, for they are done with more labor and struggle; but they are not so agreeable to the person who does them, since — not being in the sensible part of the soul — they are not so much felt, nor are they so pleasant to us.

My dearest daughter, we must not be unjust and require from ourselves what is not in ourselves. When troubled in body and health, we must not exact from our souls anything more than acts of submission and the acceptance of our suffering, and holy unions of our will to the good pleasure of God, which are formed in the highest region of the spirit. And as for exterior actions, we must manage and do them as well as we can, and be satisfied with doing them, even if without heart, languidly, and heavily. To raise these languors, heavinesses, and torpors of heart, and to make them serve toward divine love, you must profess, accept, and love holy abjection. Thus shall you change into gold the lead of your heaviness, and into gold finer than would be the gold of your most lively gladnesses of heart. Have patience then with yourself. Let your superior part bear the disorder of the inferior; and often offer to the eternal glory of our Creator the little creature in whose formation He has willed to make you His fellow worker.

My dearest daughter, we have here at Annecy a Capuchin painter who, as you may think, only paints for God and His temple. And although while working he has to pay so close an attention that he cannot pray at the same time, and although this occupies and even fatigues his spirit, still he does this work with good heart for the glory of our Lord, and with the hope that these pictures will excite many faithful to praise God and to bless His goodness.

My dear daughter, the child who is taking shape in your womb will be a living image of the divine majesty; but while your soul, your strength, and your natural vigor is occupied with this work of pregnancy, it must grow weary and tired, and you cannot at the same time perform your ordinary exercises so actively and so gaily. But suffer lovingly this lassitude and heaviness, in consideration of the honor that God will receive from your work. It is your image that will be placed in the eternal temple of the heavenly Jerusalem, and that will be eternally regarded with pleasure by God, by angels, and by men. The saints will praise God for it, and you also will praise Him when you see it there.

And so in the meantime have patience, although feeling your heart a little torpid and sluggish, and with the superior part attach yourself to the holy will of our Lord, who has so arranged for it according to His eternal wisdom.

I do not know of anything that my soul fails to think and to desire for the perfection of yours, which, as God has willed and wills it so, is truly in the midst of mine. May it please His divine goodness that both your soul and mine may be according to His most holy and good pleasure, and that all your dear family may be filled with His sacred benedictions, and especially your very dear husband, of whom, as of you, I am invariably

Your very humble and most obedient servant,

Francis

"If you get tired kneeling, sit down"

To a pregnant woman,
on loving God in her suffering

My dearest daughter,

. . . It is necessary before all things, my daughter, to obtain tranquillity, not because it is the mother of contentment, but because it is the daughter of the love of God and of the resignation of our own will.

The opportunities of practicing it are daily. For contradictions are not wanting wherever we are; and when nobody else makes them, we make them for ourselves. My God! How holy, my dear daughter, and how agreeable to God we should be, if we knew how to use properly the subjects of mortification that our vocation affords! For they are without doubt greater than among religious; the evil is that we do not make use of them as they do.

Be careful to spare yourself in this pregnancy: make no effort to oblige yourself to any kind of exercise, except quite gently. If you get tired kneeling, sit down; if you cannot command attention to pray half an hour, pray only fifteen minutes or even half of that.

I beg you to put yourself in the presence of God, and to suffer your pains before Him. Do not keep yourself from complaining; but this should be to Him, in a filial spirit, as a little child to its mother. For if it is done lovingly, there is no danger in complaining, nor in begging cure, nor in changing place, nor in getting ourselves relieved. But do this with love, and with resignation into the arms of the good will of God.

Do not trouble yourself about not making acts of virtue properly; for as I have said, they do not cease to be very good, even if they are made in a languid, heavy, and (as it were) *forced* manner.

You can only give God what you have, and in this time of affliction you have no other actions. At present, my dear daughter, your Beloved is to you a "bundle of myrrh";[50] cease not to press Him close to your breast. "My Beloved is mine, and I am His";[51] ever shall He be in my heart. Isaiah the prophet calls Him the "man of sorrows."[52] He loves sorrows, and those who have them.

Do not torment yourself to do much, but suffer with love what you have to suffer. God will be gracious to you, Madame, and will give you the grace to arrange this more retired life of which you speak to me. Whether languishing "or living or dying, we are the Lord's"[53] and nothing, with the help of His

[50] Song of Sol. 1:12.
[51] Ibid. 2:16.
[52] Isa. 53:3.
[53] Rom. 14:8.

grace, will separate us from this holy love. Never shall our heart live, save in Him and for Him; He shall be for ever "the God of our heart."[54] I will never cease to beg this of Him, nor to be entirely in Him

Your very affectionate servant,

Francis

[54] Cf. Ps. 72:26 (RSV = Ps. 73:26).

25

"You will not lack mortifications"

To a pregnant woman,
telling her to eat properly

My dearest daughter,

I am just leaving, and hence pressed for time. You must please consider these four lines as if they were many. Be sure, I beg you, that your very dear soul will never be more loved than it is by mine.

But what am I told?

They tell me that although you are pregnant, you fast, and rob your child of the nourishment that its mother requires in order to supply it.

Do it no more, I beseech you; and humbling yourself under the advice of your doctors, nourish without scruple your body, in consideration of that which you bear. You will not lack mortifications for the heart, which is the only holocaust God desires from you.

O my God! What grand souls have I found here in the service of God! May His goodness be blessed for it. And you,

Thy Will Be Done

too, are united with these souls, since you have the same desires. Live entirely in God, my dear daughter, and persevere in praying for

Your very humble brother and servant,

Francis

26

"We must always walk faithfully"

To a childless woman

My dearest daughter,

Since you have given all to God, seek nothing but Him, who is doubtless Himself the good you have received in exchange for the poor little all you have given Him. Oh, how this will increase your courage, and make you walk confidently and simply! Also, it is well to think always that your sterility comes from your fault, yet without occupying yourself in thinking what the fault is; for this thought will make you walk in humility.

Do you think, my dear daughter, that Sara, Rebecca, Rachel, Anne (the mother of Samuel), St. Anne (the mother of our Lady), and St. Elizabeth were less agreeable to God when they were barren than when they were fruitful? We must walk faithfully in the way of our Lord, and remain in peace as much in the winter of sterility as in the autumn of fruitfulness.

Our sisters are consoled by the hope of peace. They deserve to be all the more consoled by the word of the heavenly Spouse, who preserves those who are His own "as the apple of

Thy Will Be Done

His eye."[55] St. Jerome said to one of his spiritual daughters that he who walks upon the earth has no need of a plank; he who is covered by the heavens has no need of a roof.[56] Will God, who makes houses for the snails and turtles, who neither think of Him nor sing His praises, leave without a convent His servants who assemble for His praise?

My daughter, I am more and more entirely

Your very humble servant,

Francis

---

[55] Deut. 32:10.

[56] St. Jerome, Letter 43 *ad Marcellam*.

27

"Illness can make you agreeable to God"

To a woman who is ill,
on resignation to troublesome things

My dear daughter,

I understand that you have an illness more troublesome than dangerous, and I know that such illnesses are prone to spoil the obedience we owe to doctors.

For this reason, I tell you not to deprive yourself of the rest, or the medicines, or the food, or the recreations that are prescribed for you. You can exercise a kind of obedience and resignation in accepting these that will make you extremely agreeable to our Lord.

Also, consider in this illness the number of crosses and mortifications that you have neither chosen nor wished. God has given them to you with His holy hand; receive them, kiss them, love them. My God! They are all perfumed with the dignity of the place from which they come.

Goodbye, my dearest daughter, I cherish you earnestly. If I had the leisure I would say more, for I am infinitely pleased that you are faithful in these little and troublesome occurrences, and that in little things as in great ones you say always *Vive Jésus!*

Your devoted and very affectionate servant,

Francis

28

"You are being crowned with His crown of thorns"

*To a woman suffering
great physical pain*

My dear daughter,

Let us leave meditation for a short time (it is only to spring better that we step back) and let us practice well that holy resignation and that pure love of our Lord that is never entirely practiced save in troubles. To love God in sugar — little children would do as much. But to love Him in wormwood, that is the test of our amorous fidelity. To say *Vive Jésus* on the mountain of Tabor, St. Peter, while still carnal, has courage enough; but to say *Vive Jésus* on Mount Calvary — this belongs only to the Mother, and to the beloved disciple who was left to her as her son.

So then, my daughter, behold I commend you to God, to obtain for you that sacred patience; and I cannot ask Him anything for you except that He would fashion your heart in total accordance with His will, in order to lodge and reign therein eternally. Whether He do it with the hammer, or with the chisel, or with the brush, it is for Him to act according to His pleasure. Is it not so, my dear daughter? Is it not necessary that He do this?

I know that your pains have been increased lately, and in the same measure has my sorrow for them increased, although I praise and bless our Lord with you for His good pleasure exercised in you, making you share His holy Cross and crowning you with His crown of thorns.

But, you will say, you can hardly keep your thoughts on the pains our Lord has suffered for you, while your own pangs oppress you. Well, my dearest child, you are not obliged to do so, provided that you quite simply offer up your heart as frequently as you are able to this Savior, and make the following acts:

First, accept the pain from His hand, as if you saw Him Himself putting and pressing it on your head.

Second, offer yourself to suffer more.

Third, beg our Savior by the merit of His torments to accept these little distresses in union with the pains He suffered on the Cross.

Next, protest that you wish not only to suffer, but to love and cherish these sufferings since they are sent from so good and so sweet a hand.

Lastly, invoke the martyrs and the many servants of God, who enjoy Heaven as a result of their having been afflicted in this world.

It is not dangerous to desire a cure. Indeed you must carefully seek one; for God, who has given you the evil, is also author of its cure. You must then apply it, yet with such resignation that, if His divine majesty wishes the evil to conquer, you will acquiesce, and if He wishes the remedy to succeed, you will bless Him for it.

There is no harm, while performing your spiritual exercises, in being seated. None at all, my daughter; nor would there be for difficulties much less than those you suffer.

How happy you will be, my daughter, if you continue to keep yourself under the hand of God, humbly, sweetly, and pliantly! Ah! I hope this headache will much profit your heart — your heart, which mine cherishes with quite a special love. Now, my daughter, it is that you may, more than ever, and by very good signs, prove to our sweet Savior that it is with all your affection that you have said and will say *Vive Jésus! Vive Jésus!* my child, and may He reign amid your pains, since we ourselves can neither reign nor live save by the pain of His death.

I am in Him entirely

Yours,

Francis

29

"Often the world calls evil what is good"

To a woman whose husband is ill

My dearest daughter,

Truly, if charity allowed, I could willingly love the maladies of your dear husband because I think them useful to you for the mortification of your affection and feelings. Well then, leave it to be seen by the heavenly and eternal Providence of our Lord whether these illnesses will be for the good of your soul or of his, both being exercised as they are by means of holy patience.

O my child, how often the world calls *good* what is evil, and still oftener *evil* what is good!

However, since that sovereign goodness who wills our troubles wills also that we ask from Him deliverance from them, I will entreat Him with all my heart to give back good and lasting health to your dear husband, and a very excellent and very lasting holiness to you, my dearest daughter, that you may walk steadily and fervently in the way of true and living devotion. . . .

Thy Will Be Done

There seems to be illness everywhere, but illness that is a great good, as I hope. Let the good pleasure of the divine majesty ever be our pleasure and comfort in the adversities that come upon us. Amen.

Francis

30

"Rest in the arms of Providence"

To a woman facing the death of her child

My very dear mother,

We must await the result of this sickness as quietly as we can, with a perfect resolution to conform ourselves to the divine will in this loss — if absence for such a little time can be called *loss*, which, God helping, will be made up by an eternal presence.

Oh! How happy is the heart that loves and cherishes the divine will in all events!

Oh! If only we have our hearts closely united to that holy and happy eternity! "Go" — we shall say to all our friends — "go, dear friends, go into that eternal existence at the time fixed by the king of eternity; we shall follow after you." And as this time on earth is only given us for that purpose, and as this world is only peopled to people Heaven, when we go there we do all that we have to do. This is the reason why, my mother, our ancestors have so much admired the sacrifice of

Abraham.[57] What a father's heart! They admired, too, your holy countrywoman, the mother of St. Symphorian, with whose holy act I finish my book![58] Oh God, my mother, let us leave our children to the mercy of God, who has left His Son to our mercy. Let us offer to Him the life of our child, as He has given for us the life of His. In general, we should keep our eyes fixed on heavenly Providence, in whose dispensations we ought to acquiesce with all the humility of our heart.

God bless you, and mark your heart with the eternal sign of His pure love! Very humbly, we must become saints, and spread everywhere the good and sweet odor of our charity. May God make us burn with His holy love and despise all for that! May our Lord be the repose of our heart and of our body! Every day I learn not to do my own will and to do what I do not want. Rest in peace in the two arms of divine Providence, and in the bosom of the protection of our Lady.

Francis

---

[57] Gen. 22:1-12.
[58] *Introduction to the Devout Life*, Part 5, ch. 18.

31

"In confidence, lift up your heart to our Redeemer"

*To a woman, on how to
conquer the fear of death*

Madame,

On this first opportunity that I have of writing to you, I keep
my promise, and present you some means for softening the fear
of death that gives you such great terrors in your sicknesses and
childbearings. In this fear there is no sin, but still there is
damage to your heart, which cannot, troubled by this passion,
in love join itself so well to its God, as it would do if it were
not so tormented.

I assure you, then, that if you persevere in the exercise of
devotion, as I see you do, you will find yourself, little by little,
much relieved of this torment; so that your soul, thus exempt
from evil affections and uniting itself more and more with
God, will find itself less attached to this mortal life and to the
empty satisfactions that it gives.

Continue, then, the devout life, as you have begun, and go
always from well to better in the road in which you are; and

you will see that after some time these errors will grow weak and will not trouble you so much.

Exercise yourself often in the thoughts of the great sweetness and mercy with which God our Savior receives souls in their death when they have trusted themselves to Him in their life and when they have tried to serve and love Him, each one in his vocation. "How good art Thou, Lord, to them that are of a right heart."[59]

Frequently lift up your heart by a holy confidence, mingled with a profound humility toward our Redeemer, saying as you do: "I am miserable, Lord, and You will receive my misery into the bosom of Your mercy, and You will draw me, with Your paternal hand, to the enjoyment of Your eternal inheritance. I am frail, and vile, and abject; nevertheless, You will love me in that day, because I have hoped in You, and have desired to be Yours."

Excite in yourself as much as possible the love of Paradise and of the celestial life, and make some considerations on this subject, which you will find sufficiently marked in the *Introduction to the Devout Life*, in the meditations on the glory of Heaven and the choice of Paradise.[60] For in proportion as you esteem eternal happiness, you will have less fear of leaving this mortal and perishable life.

Read no books or parts of books in which death, judgment, and Hell are spoken of, for, thanks to God, you have quite resolved to live in a Christian manner, and have no need to be driven to it by motives of terror and fear.

[59] Cf. Ps. 72:1 (RSV = Ps. 73:1).

[60] *Introduction to the Devout Life*, Part 1, chs. 16-17.

Lift up your heart to our Redeemer

Often make acts of love toward our Lady, the saints, and the angels. Make yourself familiar with them, and often address to them words of praise and love; for having close relations with the citizens of the divine, heavenly Jerusalem, it will trouble you less to quit those of the earthly or lower city of the world.

Often adore, praise, and bless the most holy death of our Lord crucified, and place all your trust in His merit, by which your death will be made happy, and often say: "O divine death of my sweet Jesus, Thou shalt bless mine and it shall be blessed; I bless Thee and Thou shalt bless me. O death more dear than life!" Thus St. Charles[61] in his last illness had placed in his sight the picture of Christ's tomb and of His prayer in the garden, so that he might console himself in his moment of death by the death and Passion of his Redeemer.

Reflect, sometimes, that you are a daughter of the Church, and rejoice in this. For the children of this mother who are willing to live according to Her laws always die happily; and as the blessed St. Teresa says, it is a great consolation at death to have been a child of Holy Church.[62]

Finish all your prayers in hope, saying, "O Lord, Thou art my hope;[63] my soul trusteth in Thee."[64] Ask: "My God, who has hoped in Thee and been confounded?"[65] "In Thee, O Lord,

---

[61] St. Charles Borromeo (1538-1604), one of the leaders of the Catholic Counter-Reformation of the sixteenth century.

[62] Francisco de Ribera (1537-1591), *The Life of Mother Teresa*, Bk. 3, ch. 15.

[63] Ps. 141:6 (RSV = Ps. 142:5).

[64] Ps. 56:2 (RSV = Ps. 57:1).

[65] Cf. Ecclus. 2:11 (RSV = Sirach 2:10).

have I hoped, let me never be confounded."[66] In your prayer during the day and in receiving the Blessed Sacrament, always use words of love and hope toward our Lord, such as: "You are my Father, O Lord! O God! You are the Spouse of my soul, the King of my love and the well beloved of my soul! O good Jesus, you are my dear Master, my aid, my refuge!

Consider often that the persons whom you love most, and from whom separation would trouble you, are the persons with whom you will be eternally in Heaven: for instance, your husband, your little John, and your father. Oh! This little boy will be, God helping, one day happy in that eternal life in which he will enjoy my happiness and rejoice over it; and I shall enjoy his and rejoice over it, and we shall never more be separated! So of your husband, your father, and others. You will find it all the more easy because all your dearest serve God. And since you are a little melancholy, see in the *Introduction* what I say there about sadness and the remedies against it.[67]

Here, my dear lady, you have what I can say on this subject for the present. I say it to you with a heart very affectionate toward yours, which I beg to love me and to recommend me often to the divine mercy, as in return I will not cease to beg the divine mercy to bless you. Live happy and joyous in heavenly love, and I am

Your most humble servant,

Francis

[66] Ps. 30:1 (RSV = Ps. 31:1).

[67] *Introduction to the Devout Life*, Part 4, ch. 12.

"We must slowly withdraw from the world"

---

*To an elderly man, telling
him how to prepare for death*

Sir,

. . . I know that you have passed a long and very honorable life, and have always been very constant in the Holy Catholic Church; but, after all, it has been in the world, and in the management of its affairs. It is a strange thing, but experience and authors witness it: a horse, however fine and strong he may be, travelling on the paths and trail of the wolf, becomes giddy and stumbles. It is not possible that, while living in the world, although we only touch it with our feet, we are not soiled with its dust. Thus says St. Leo.[68]

Our ancient fathers, Abraham and the others, usually offered to their guests the washing of their feet.[69] I think, sir, that the first thing to be done is to wash the affections of our souls

---

[68] St. Leo the Great, *Sermon* 42, ch. 1.
[69] Gen. 18:4.

in order to receive the hospitality of our good God in His Paradise.

It seems to me that it is always a great matter of reproach to mortals to die without having thought of this; but doubly so to those whom God has favored with the blessing of old age. Those who get ready before the alarm is given, always put on their armor better than those who, on the fright, run hither and thither for the cuirass, the cuisses, and the helmet.

We must leisurely say goodbye to the world, and little by little withdraw our affections from creatures. Trees that the wind tears up are not suitable to transplant, because they leave their roots in the earth; but he who would carry trees into another soil must skillfully disengage little by little all the roots one after the other. And since from this miserable land we are to be transplanted into that of the living, we must withdraw and disengage our affections one after the other from this world. I do not say that we must roughly break all the ties we have formed (it would, perhaps, require immense efforts for that), but we must unsew and untie them.

Those who depart suddenly are excusable for not saying goodbye to their friends, and for starting with a poor setting out; but not so those who know the probable time of their journey. They must keep ready — not, indeed, as if to start before the time, but to await it with more tranquillity.

For this purpose, I think, sir, that you will have an incredible consolation if you choose from each day an hour, to think before God and your good angel, on what is necessary to make a happy departure. What order would your affairs be in if you knew your death would be soon? I know these thoughts will not be new to you; but the way of making them must be new in the presence of God, with a tranquil attention, and rather for the purpose of moving the affections than enlightening the intellect.

St. Jerome has more than once[70] applied to the wisdom of the old the history of Abishag, the Shunammite, who slept on the bosom of David not out of sensuality but solely to warm him.[71] Wisdom and the consideration of philosophy often engage young people; it is more to recreate their spirit than to excite good movements in their affections. But wisdom and the consideration of philosophy should engage the old solely to give them the true warmth of devotion.

I have seen and enjoyed your fine library; I present you, for your spiritual lesson on this matter, St. Ambrose, *De bono mortis* (*On the benefit of death*), St. Bernard, *De interiori domo* (*On the interior house*), and several scattered homilies of St. John Chrysostom.

Your St. Bernard says that the soul should first go and kiss the feet of the crucifix, to rectify its affections, and to resolve with firm resolution to withdraw itself little by little from the world and its vanities; then kiss the hands, by that newness of actions that follows the change of affections; and finally that the soul should kiss the mouth, uniting itself by an ardent love to the supreme goodness.[72] This is the true progress of a becoming departure.

It is said that Alexander the Great, sailing on the wide ocean, discovered, alone and first, Arabia Felix, by the scent

---

[70] St. Jerome, Letter 52 *ad Nepotianum*, 2-3.

[71] 3 Kings 1:1-4 (RSV = 1 Kings 1:1-4).

[72] St. Bernard of Clairvaux, *Sermons on Diverse Matters*, 87.1.

of its aromatic trees.[73] He was at first the only one to perceive it, because he alone was seeking it. Those who seek after the eternal country, although sailing on the high sea of the affairs of this world, possess a certain presentiment of Heaven, which animates and encourages them marvelously. But they must keep themselves before the wind, and their prow turned in the proper direction.

We owe ourselves to God, to our country, to our parents, to our friends. To God, firstly; then to our country (that is, first to our heavenly country and secondly to our earthly one). Then we owe ourselves to our near ones, but "no one is so near as ourself," says our Christian Seneca.[74] Finally, we owe ourselves to friends; but are you not the first of your friends? He remarks that St. Paul says to Timothy, "Attend to yourself and to your flock"[75] — first to yourself, then to your flock.

This is quite enough, sir, if not too much, for this year, which flies and melts away before us, and in these two next months will make us see the vanity of its existence like all the preceding, which exist no more. You commanded me to write you every year something of this sort. I am now straight for this year, in which I beseech you to withdraw your affections from the world as much as possible, and in proportion as you withdraw them to transport them to Heaven.

And pardon me, I beseech you, by your own humility, if my simplicity has been so extravagant in its obedience as to write to you, at such length and freedom on a simple demand, and

[73] Pliny the Elder, *Natural History*, Book 12, ch. 42.

[74] St. Bernard of Clairvaux, *On Consideration*, Bk. 1, ch. 5.

[75] Acts 20:28.

We must draw back from the world

with the full sense that I have of your abundant wisdom, which should keep me either in silence or in an exact moderation. Here are waters, sir; if they come from the jawbone of an ass, Samson will not refuse to drink of them.[76] I pray God to heap up your years with His benedictions, and I am, with an entirely filial affection, sir,

Your most humble and obedient servant,

Francis

---

[76] Judg. 15:19.

33

"This dear child was more God's than yours"

To a man whose son has died

Sir,

Knowing what you have felt about your son by that which I have felt myself, I realize that your pain has been extreme; for truly, remembering the contentment that you took in speaking to me the other day about this child, I felt a great compassion when I reflected how painful would be your sorrow at the news of his death. But still I did not dare to express to you my sympathy, not knowing whether his loss was certain, nor whether it had been told to you.

And now, sir, I come too late to contribute toward the consolation of your heart, which will already, I am sure, have received much relief, so as no longer to remain in the grief that so deep an affliction had caused it.

For you will have well known how to consider that this dear child was more God's than yours, who had it only as a loan from that sovereign liberality. And if His Providence judged that it was time to withdraw it to Himself, we must believe

117

that it was for the child's good, in which a loving father like you must quietly acquiesce. The time in which we live is not so delightful that those who quit it should be much lamented. This son has, I think, gained much by leaving it almost before properly entering it.

The word *dead* is terrifying, as it is spoken to us; for some one comes to you and says, "Your dear father is dead," and "Your son is dead."

But this is not a fit way of speaking among us Christians, for we should say, "Your son or your father has gone into his and your country"; and because it was necessary, he has passed through death, not stopping in it.

I know not, indeed, how we can in right judgment esteem this world to be our country, in which we are for so short a time, in comparison with Heaven, in which we are to be eternally.

We are on our way, and are more assured of the presence of our dear friends there above than of these here below. For our friends there in Heaven are expecting us, and we are going toward them; our friends here on earth let us go, and will linger as long after us as they can; and if they go with us, it is against their will.

But if some remains of sorrow still oppress your mind for the departure of this sweet soul, throw your heart before our Lord crucified, and ask His help. He will give it to you, and will inspire in you the thought and the firm resolution to prepare yourself well to make this terrifying passage in your turn at the hour He has fixed, in such way that you may happily arrive at the place in which we hope already is lodged our poor — or rather our happy — departed.

This child was more God's than yours

Sir, if I am heard in my continual desire, you will be filled with all holy prosperity; for it is with all my heart that I cherish and honor yours; and in this occasion, and in every other, I name myself and make myself, sir,

Your very humble and obedient servant,

Francis

34

"Think of no other place than Paradise or Purgatory"

*To a woman anxious about
the fate of her deceased son*

My dearest mother,

Having received your letter, I will tell you that I know dis-
tinctly the qualities of your heart, and above all its ardor and
strength in loving and cherishing what it loves. It is this that
makes you speak so much to our Lord of your dear departed,
and which impels you to these desires of knowing where he is.

But, my dear mother, you must repress these longings that
proceed from the excess of this amorous passion; and when you
discover your mind in this occupation, you must immediately,
and even with vocal prayers, return to our Lord, and say to
Him this or the like: "O Lord, how sweet is Your Providence!
How good is Your mercy! Ah! How happy is this child to have
fallen into Your fatherly arms, where he cannot but have good,
wherever he is!"

Yes, my dear mother, for you must take great care to think
of no other place than Paradise or Purgatory. Thank God,

there is no cause to think otherwise. In this way, draw back, then, thus your mind, and afterward turn it to actions of love for our Lord crucified.

And when you recommend your child to the divine majesty, say to God simply, "Lord, I commend to You the child of my womb, but much more the child of Your mercy, born of my blood, but born again of Yours."

And then pass on: for if you permit your soul to dwell on this object, adapted and agreeable to its senses and to its inferior and natural powers, it will never be willing to tear itself away; and under pretence of prayers of piety it will give itself up to certain natural complacencies and satisfactions, which will deprive you of time to employ yourself with the supernatural and sovereign object of your love. You must certainly moderate these ardors of natural affection, which only serve to trouble our mind and distract our heart.

So, then, my dearest mother, whom I love with a truly filial love, let us withdraw our mind into our heart, and bring it to its duty of loving God most solely; let us allow it no frivolous preoccupation, either about what passes in this world or in the other. But having given to creatures what we owe them of love and charity, let us refer all to that primary, mastering love that we owe to our Creator, and let us conform ourselves to His divine will. I am, very affectionately, my dear mother,

Your most faithful and affectionate child,

Francis

35

"How tenderly I loved her!"

To Jane de Chantal, on the
death of Francis's younger sister

My dear daughter,

Ah, well, is it not reasonable that the most holy will of God should be done, as much in the things we cherish as in others? But I must hasten to tell you that my good mother has drunk this chalice with an entirely Christian constancy, and her virtue, of which I had always a high opinion, has far exceeded my estimation.

On Sunday morning, she sent for my brother the Canon; and because she had seen him very sad, and all the other brothers as well, the night before, she began by saying to him, "I have dreamt all the night that my daughter Jane is dead. Tell me, I beseech you, is it not true?" My brother, who was awaiting my arrival to break it to her (for I was on my episcopal visitation), saw this good opening for presenting the chalice to her. "It is true, mother," he said, and no more, for he had not strength to add anything. "God's will be done," said my good mother, and wept abundantly for some space; and then, calling her maid Nicole, she said, "I want to get up and go pray to God in the chapel for my poor daughter," and immediately did what she said. Not a single word of impatience, not a look of disquiet; but blessings of God, and a thousand resignations in her will. Never did I see a calmer grief; such tears that it was a marvel, but all from simple tenderness of heart, without any sort of passion, even though it was her own dear child. Ah! Should I not then love this mother well?

Yesterday, All Saints' Day, I was the grand confessor of the family, and with the most Holy Sacrament I scaled the heart of this mother against all sadness. For the rest, she thanks you infinitely for the care and maternal love which you have shown toward this deceased little one, with as much obligation to you as if God had preserved her by your means. My brothers say as much, who in truth have manifested extremely good dispositions in this affliction, especially our Boisy, whom I love the more for it.

I well know that you would gladly ask me, "And you, how did you bear yourself?" Yes, for you want to know how I am doing. Ah, my child, I am as human as I can be; my heart was grieved more than I should ever have thought. But the truth is that the pain to my mother and your pain have greatly increased mine; for I have feared for your heart, and my mother's. But as for the rest, *vive Jésus*, I will always take the side of divine Providence: it does all well, and disposes all things for the best. What happiness for this dear child to have been "taken away, lest wickedness should alter her understanding,"[77] and to have left this miry place before she had

[77] Wisd. of Sol. 4:11.

gotten soiled therein! We gather strawberries and cherries before apples and oranges, but it is because their season requires it. Let God gather what He has planted in His orchard: He takes everything in its season.

You may think, my dear daughter, how tenderly I loved this little child. I had brought her forth to her Savior, for I had baptized her with my own hand, some fourteen years ago. She was the first creature on whom I exercised my order of priesthood. I was her spiritual father, and fully promised myself one day to make out of her something good. And what made her all the more dear to me (and I speak the truth) was that she was yours.[78]

But still, my dear child, in the midst of my heart of flesh, which has had such keen feelings about this death, I perceive deep within a certain sweetness, tranquillity, and a certain gentle repose of my spirit in divine Providence, which spreads abroad in my heart a great contentment in its pains.

Here, then, are my feelings represented as far as I can. But you, what do you mean when you tell me that you found yourself on this occasion such as you were? Tell me, I beseech you: was not the needle of your compass always turning to its bright pole, to its holy star, to its God? Your heart — what has it been doing? Have you scandalized those who saw you in this matter and in this event? Now this, my dear child, tell me clearly; for, do you see, it was not right to offer either your own life or that of one of your other children in exchange for that of the departed one. No, my dear child, we must not only

---

[78] Jane de Sales was living with St. Jane de Chantal at the time of her death.

consent for God to strike us, but we must let it be in the place which He pleases. We must leave the choice to God, for it belongs to Him. David offered his life for that of his Absalom, but it was because Absalom died reprobate.[79] In such cases we must beseech God, but in temporal loss — O my daughter, let God touch and strike whatever string of our lute He chooses; He will never make anything but a good harmony. Lord Jesus! Without reserve, without *if*, without *but*, without exception, without limitation, Your will be done, in father, in mother, in daughter, in all and everywhere! Ah! I do not say that we must not wish and pray for their preservation; but we must not say to God, "Leave this and take that"; my dear child, we must not say so. And we will not, will we? No, no; no, my child, by help of the grace of His divine goodness.

I seem to see you, my dear child, with your vigorous heart, which loves and wills powerfully. I congratulate it thereon: for what are these half-dead hearts good for? But it behooves us to make a particular exercise, once every week, of willing and loving the will of God more vigorously, (I go further) more tenderly, more amorously, than anything in the world; and this not only in bearable occurrences, but in the most unbearable. You will find more than I can describe in the little book of the *Spiritual Combat*, which I have so often recommended to you.

Ah, my child, to speak the truth, this lesson is sublime; but so also God, for whom we learn it, is the most sublime. You have, my child, four children; you have a father-in-law, a dear brother, and then again a spiritual father: all these are very dear to you, and rightly; for God wills it. Well, now, if God

[79] 2 Kings 18:33 (RSV = 2 Sam. 18:33).

took all this from you, would you not still have enough in having God? Is that not *all*, in your estimation? If we had nothing else but God, would it not be enough?

Alas! The Son of God, my dear Jesus, had scarce so much on the Cross, when, having given up and left all for love and obedience to His Father, He was as if left and given up by Him; and, as the torrent of His passion swept off His bark to desolation, hardly did He perceive the needle, which was not only turned toward, but inseparably joined with, His Father. Yes, He was one with His Father, but the inferior part knew and perceived nothing of it whatever: a trial which the divine goodness has made and will make in no other soul, for no other soul could bear it.

Well then, my child, if God takes everything from us, He will never take Himself from us, so long as we do not will it. But more; all our losses and our separations are but for this little moment. Oh truly, for so little a time as this, we ought to have patience.

I pour myself out, it seems to me, a little too much. But why? I follow my heart, which never feels it says too much with this dear daughter. I send you the family coat of arms to satisfy you. Since it pleases you to have the funeral services where this child rests in the body, I am willing; but without great pomp, beyond what Christian custom requires: what good is the rest?

You will afterward draw out a list of all these expenses, as well as those of her illness, and send it to me, for I wish it so; and meantime we shall beseech God here for this soul, and will properly do its little honors. We shall not send for its forty days' remembrance; no, my child, so much ceremony is not becoming for a child who has had no rank in this world; it would get one laughed at. You know me: I love simplicity both in life and in death. I shall be very glad to know the name and the title of the church where she is. This is all I have to say on this subject. . . .

Your very affectionate servant,

Francis

36

"Calm your mind, lift up your heart"

To a woman whose husband died recently

Madame,

You cannot think how deeply I feel your affliction. For many reasons, but chiefly for his virtue and piety, I honored with a very particular affection this dear departed gentleman. How grievous that, at a time when there is so great a dearth of such souls among men of his rank, we should see and suffer these losses, so injurious to the commonwealth.

Still, my dear lady, considering all things, we must accommodate our hearts to the condition of life in which we are. This is a perishing and mortal life, and death, which rules over this life, keeps no regular course — it seizes sometimes here, sometimes there, without choice or any method, the good among the bad, and the young among the old.

Oh, how happy are they who, being always on their guard against death, find themselves always ready to die, so that they may live again eternally in the life where there is no more death! Our beloved dead was of this number, I well know. That alone, Madame, is enough to console us; for at last, after a few days, or sooner or later in a few years, we shall follow him in this passage; and the friendships and fellowships begun in this world will be taken up again never to be broken off. Meanwhile, until the hour of our departure strikes, let us have patience and await with courage our own departure for that place where these friends already are. And as we have loved them cordially, let us continue to love them, doing for their love what they wished us to do in the past, and what they now wish for on our behalf.

Doubtless, my dear lady, the greatest desire your deceased husband had at his departure was that you should not long remain in the grief that his absence would cause you, but try to moderate, for love of him, the passion that love of him excited in you. And now in the happiness that he enjoys, or certainly expects, he wishes you a holy consolation, and that by moderating your tribulation, you save your eyes for a better purpose than tears, and your mind for a more desirable occupation than sorrow.

He has left you precious pledges of your marriage. Keep your eyes to look after their bringing up; keep your mind to raise up theirs. Do this, Madame, for the love of your dear husband, and imagine that he asked you for this at his departure, and still requires this service from you. For truly he would have done it if he could, and he now desires it. The rest of your griefs may be according to your heart, which remains in this world, but not according to his, which is in the other.

And since true friendship delights in satisfying the just desires of the friend, so now in order to please your husband, be consoled; calm your mind, and lift up your heart. And if this counsel that I give you with entire sincerity is agreeable to you, put it into practice. Prostrate yourself before your Savior, acquiesce in His ordinance; consider the soul of this dear departed, which wishes from yours a true and Christian resolution; and abandon yourself altogether to the heavenly Providence of the Savior of your soul, your protector, who will help you and succor you, and will, in the end, unite you with your dead, not as wife with husband but as heiress of Heaven with co-heir, and as faithful lover with her beloved.

I write this, Madame, without leisure and almost without breath, offering you that very loving service of mine that has long been yours, and also that is required from my soul by the merits and the goodness of your husband toward me.

God be in the midst of your heart. Amen.

Francis

37

"Miserable beggars receive the greatest mercy"

To Jane de Chantal,
on humility and widowhood

My dear sister,

My God! What heartiness and passion I have in the service of your soul! You could not sufficiently believe it. I have so much that this alone suffices to convince me that it is from our Lord. For it is not possible, I think, that all the world together could give me so much — at least, I have never seen so much in the world. I give this letter to this carrier because he will be coming back, and will be able to bring me your letters.

Today is the feast of All Saints, and at our solemn Matins, seeing our Lord begin the Beatitudes with poverty of spirit, which St. Augustine interprets as the holy and most desirable virtue of humility,[80] I remembered that you had asked me to send you something about humility. I think I said nothing about it in my last letter, although it was very ample and

---

[80] St. Augustine, *On the Sermon on the Mount,* Bk. 1, ch. 1.

perhaps too long. Now, God has given me so many things to write to you, that if I had time, I think I should say wonders.

In the first place, my dearest sister, it comes to my mind that learned men attribute to widows, as their proper virtue, holy humility. Virgins have theirs, so have martyrs, scholars, pastors — each his or her own, like the order of their knighthood. And all must have had humility, for they would not have been exalted had they not been humbled. But to widows belongs, before all, humility; for what can puff up the widow with pride?

The widow no longer has her virginity. (This can, however, be amply compensated by a great widowly humility. It is much better to be a widow with plenty of oil in our lamp, by desiring nothing but humility and charity, than to be a virgin without oil or with little oil.)[81]

The widow no longer has that which gives the highest value to your sex in the estimation of the world; she has no longer her husband, who was her honor, and whose name she has taken.

What more remains to glorify herself in, except God? O happy glory! O precious crown! In the garden of the Church, widows are compared to violets, little and low flowers, of no striking color nor of very intense perfume, but marvelously sweet. Oh, how lovely a flower is the Christian widow, little and low by humility! She is not brilliant in the eyes of the world; for she avoids them, and no longer adorns herself to draw them on her. And why should she desire the eyes when she no longer desires the hearts?

[81] Cf. Matt. 25:3.

The miserable receive great mercy

The Apostle orders his dear disciple to "honor the widows who are widows indeed."[82] And who are "widows indeed" save those who are such in heart and mind — that is, who have their heart married to no creature? Our Lord does not say "blessed are the clean of body," but rather the clean "of heart"; and He praises not "the poor," but "the poor in spirit."[83] Widows are to be honored when they are such in heart and mind; what does *widow* mean except "deserted and forlorn" — that is, miserable, poor, and little? Those, then, who are poor, miserable, and little in mind and heart, are to be praised. All this means those who are humble, of whom our Lord is the protector.

But what is humility? Is it the knowledge of this misery and poverty? Yes, says our St. Bernard, but this is moral and human humility.[84]

What then is Christian humility? It is the love of this poverty and abjection, contemplating these in our Lord. You know that you are a very wretched and weak widow? Love this miserable state; make it your glory to be nothing. Be glad of it, since your misery becomes an object for the goodness of God to show His mercy in.

Among beggars, those who are the most miserable and whose sores are the largest and most loathsome, think themselves the best beggars and the most likely to draw alms. We are but beggars; the most miserable are the best off. The mercy of God willingly looks on them.

---

[82] 1 Tim. 5:3.

[83] Matt. 5:8.

[84] St. Bernard of Clairvaux, *Sermon on the Advent of Our Lord*, 4.4.

Thy Will Be Done

Let us humble ourselves, I beseech you, and plead only our sores and miseries at the gate of the divine mercy; but remember to plead them with joy, comforting yourself in being completely empty, and completely a widow, that our Lord may fill you with His kingdom. Be mild and affable with every one, except with those who would take away your glory, which is your wretchedness and your perfect widowhood. "I glory in my infirmities," says the Apostle, and "it is better for me to die than lose my glory."[85] Do you see? He would rather die than lose his infirmities, which are his glory!

You must carefully guard your misery and your littleness; for God regards it, as He did that of the Blessed Virgin. "Man seeth those things that appear, but the Lord beholdeth the heart."[86] If He sees our littleness in our hearts, He will give us great graces. This humility preserves chastity, for which reason, in the Song of Solomon that lovely soul is called the "lily of the valleys."[87]

Be then joyously humble before God, but be joyously humble also before the world. Be very glad that the world takes no account of you; if it esteems you, mock at it gaily, and laugh at its judgment, and at your misery that is judged. If it esteems you not, console yourself joyously, because in this, at least, the world follows truth.

As for the exterior, do not affect visible humility, but also do not run away from it; embrace it, and ever joyously. I approve the lowering of ourselves sometimes to mean offices,

[85] 2 Cor. 12:9.
[86] 1 Kings 16:7 (RSV = 1 Sam. 16:7).
[87] Song of Sol. 2:1.

even toward inferiors and proud persons, toward the sick and the poor, toward our own people at home and abroad; but it must always be ingenuously and joyously. I repeat it often, because it is the key of this mystery for you and for me. I might rather have said "charitably," for charity, says St. Bernard, is joyous;[88] and this he says after St. Paul.[89] Humble services and matters of exterior humility are only the rind, but this preserves the fruit.

Continue your Communions and exercises, as I have written to you. Keep your soul very closely this year to meditation on the life and death of our Lord. It is the gate of Heaven; if you keep His company you will learn His disposition. Have a great and long-suffering courage; do not lose it for mere noise, and especially not in temptations against the Faith.

Our enemy is a great clatterer; do not trouble yourself at all about him. He cannot hurt you, I well know. Mock at him and let him go on. Do not fight with him; ridicule him, for it is all nothing. He has howled round about the saints, and made plenty of hubbub, but to what purpose? In spite of it all, there they are, seated in the place that he has lost, the wretch!

I want you to look at the forty-first chapter of the *Way of Perfection* by the blessed St. Teresa, for it will help you to understand well the doctrine that I have told you so often, that we must not be too minute in the exercises of virtues, that we must walk openheartedly, frankly, naïvely, after the old fashion, with liberty, in good faith, in a broad way. I fear the spirit of constraint and melancholy. No, my dear child, I desire that

---

[88] St. Bernard of Clairvaux, *Treatise on Charity*, ch. 9.
[89] Gal. 5:22.

you should have a heart large and noble, in the way of our Lord, but humble, gentle, and without laxness.

I commend myself to the little but penetrating prayers of our Celse-Bénigne; and if Aimée[90] begins to give me some little wishes, I shall hold them very dear. I give you, and your widow's heart, and your children, every day to our Lord, when offering His Son. Pray for me, my dear child, that one day we may see one another with all the saints in Paradise. My desire to love you and to be loved by you has no less measure than eternity. May the sweet Jesus will to give us this in His love and direction! Amen.

I am then, and wish to be eternally, entirely

Yours in Jesus Christ,

Francis

---

[90] St. Jane de Chantal's son and daughter.

Bearing Your Cross

———

38

"Love God crucified, even amid darkness"

*To Jane de Chantal, on bearing
abjection, and even loving it*

My dearest daughter,

May God assist me to answer properly your letter of the ninth of July. I greatly desire to do so, but I foresee clearly I shall not have leisure enough to arrange my thoughts; it will be much if I can express them.

You are right, my child; speak with me frankly, as if you were with me — that is, with a soul that God, of His sovereign authority, has made all yours.

You begin to put your hand to the work a little, you tell me. Ah! My God, what a great consolation for me! Do this always; always put your hand to the work a little. Spin every day some little, either in the day, by the light of interior influences and brightness, or in the night, by the light of the lamp, in help-lessness and sterility.

The wise man in the book of Proverbs praises the valiant woman because, he says, "her fingers have taken hold of the spindle."[91] I willingly say to you something on this word. Your distaff is the heap of your desires; spin each day a little, draw out your plans into execution, and you will certainly do well. But beware of eager haste; for you will twist your thread into knots and stop your spindle. Let us always be moving; however slowly we advance, we shall make plenty of way.

Your powerlessness hurts you greatly, for, you say, it keeps you from entering into yourself and approaching God. This is wrong, without doubt; God leaves this powerlessness in us for His glory and for our great benefit. He wants our misery to be the throne of His mercy, and our powerlessness the seat of His omnipotence. Where did God place the divine strength that He gave to Samson but in his hair, the weakest place in him?[92] Let me no more hear these words from a daughter who would serve her God according to His divine pleasure, and not according to her sensible taste and attraction. "Although He should kill me," says Job, "yet will I trust in Him."[93] No, my child, this powerlessness does not hinder you from entering into yourself, although it does hinder you from growing complacent about yourself.

We are always wanting this and that, and although we may have our sweet Jesus on our breast, we are not content. Yet this is all we can desire. One thing is necessary for us, which is to be with Him.

Tell me, my dearest child, you know very well that at the birth of our Lord Jesus Christ the shepherds heard the angelic

[91] Prov. 31:19.
[92] Judg. 16:17.
[93] Job 13:15.

and divine hymns of those heavenly spirits — Scripture says so.[94] Yet it is not said that our Lady and St. Joseph, who were the closest to the child, heard the voice of the angels, or saw that miraculous light. On the contrary, instead of hearing these angels sing, they heard the child weep, and saw, by a little light borrowed from some wretched lamp, the eyes of this divine child all filled with tears, and faint under the rigor of the cold.

I ask you in truth, would you not have chosen to be in the stable, dark and filled with the cries of the little baby, rather than to be with the shepherds, thrilling with joy and delight in the sweetness of this heavenly music and the beauty of this admirable light?

"Lord," said St. Peter, "it is good for us to be here,"[95] to see the Transfiguration; and today is the day on which it is celebrated in the Church, the sixth of August. But your Abbess is not there, but only on Mount Calvary, where she sees nothing but the dead, but nails, thorns, helplessness, darkness, abandonment, and dereliction.

I have said enough, my child, and more than I wished, on a subject that has already been so much discussed between us. No more, I beg you.

Love God crucified amid darkness; stay near Him. Say, "It is good for me to be here: let us make here three tabernacles" — one to our Lord, another to our Lady, the other to St. John. Three crosses, and no more. Take your stand by that of the Son, or that of the Mother, your Abbess, or that of the disciple.

[94] Luke 2:13-14.
[95] Matt. 17:4.

Thy Will Be Done

Everywhere you will be well received with the other daughters of your order, who are there all round about.

Love your abjection. But, you will say, "what does this mean, 'love your abjection'? My understanding is dark and powerless for any good." Well, my child, that is just the thing: if you remain humble, tranquil, gentle, and confiding amid this darkness and powerlessness; if you do not grow impatient, do not excite yourself, do not distress yourself on this account, but with good heart (I do not say gaily, but I do say sincerely and firmly) embrace this cross, and stay in this darkness, *then* you love your own abjection. For what else is it to be abject, than to be amid darkness and powerless? Love to be such as this for the love of Him who wishes you to be so, and you will love your own abjection.

My child, in Latin abjection is called *humility* and humility *abjection*, so that when our Lady says, "Because He hath had regard to the humility of His handmaid,"[96] she means, "Because He hath had regard to my abjection and vileness." Still there is some difference between humility and abjection, in that humility is the acknowledgment of one's abjection. Now the highest point of humility is not only to know one's abjection, but to love it; and it is this to which I have exhorted you.

In order that I may make myself better understood, know that among the evils that we suffer, there are evils abject and evils honorable; many accept the honorable ones, few the abject. For example, look at that Capuchin, in rags and starved with cold; everybody honors his torn habit, and has compassion on his suffering. Look at a poor artisan, a poor scholar, a

[96] Luke 1:48.

poor widow, who is in the same state; they are laughed at, and their poverty is abject.

A religious suffers patiently a rebuke from his superior; everybody calls this mortification and obedience. A gentleman will suffer such for the love of God; it will be called cowardice. Here is an abject virtue, suffering despised. One man has a cancer on his arm, another on his face. The first hides it, and only has the evil; the other cannot hide it, and with the evil he has contempt and abjection. Now, I am saying that we must love not only the evil, but also the abjection.

Further, there are abject virtues and honorable virtues. Ordinarily patience, gentleness, mortification, and simplicity are, among seculars, abject virtues; to give alms, to be courteous, to be prudent, are honorable virtues.

Of the actions of one and the same virtue, some may be abject, others honorable. To give alms and to pardon injuries are actions of charity; the first is honorable, and the other is abject in the eyes of the world.

Suppose I am ill among people who make it a burden to them: here is abjection joined with the evil. Young married ladies of the world, seeing me in the dress of a true widow, say that I play the saint, and seeing me laugh, although modestly, they say that I still wish to be sought after. They cannot believe that I do not want more honor and rank than I have, that I love my vocation without regret: all these are points of abjection. Here are some of another kind.

We go, my sisters and I, to visit the sick. My sisters send me off to visit the more miserable; this is an abjection, according to the world. They send me to visit the less miserable; this is an abjection, according to God. For the latter is the less worthy before God, and the other before the world. Now, I will love the one and the other as the occasion comes. Going to the more miserable, I will say it is quite true that I am worthless. Going to the less miserable, I will say it is very right, for I am not sufficiently worthy to make the holier visit.

I commit some folly; it makes me abject. Good. I slip down, and get into a violent passion; I am grieved at the offence to God, and very glad that this should show me vile, abject, and wretched.

At the same time, my child, take good heed of what I am going to say to you. Although we may love the abjection that follows from the evil, still we must not neglect to remedy the evil. I will do what I can not to have the cancer in the face; but if I have it, I will love the abjection of it. And in matter of sin again, we must keep to this rule. I have committed some fault; I am grieved at it, although I embrace with good heart the abjection that follows from it. And if one could be separated from the other, I would dearly cherish the abjection, and would take away the evil and sin.

Again, we must have regard to charity, which requires sometimes that we remove the abjection for the edification of our neighbor. But in that case, we must take it away from the eyes of our neighbor (who would take scandal at it), but not from our own heart, which is edified by it. "I have chosen," says the prophet, "to be abject in the house of God, rather than to dwell in the tents of sinners."[97]

Lastly, my child, you want to know which are the best abjections. I will tell you that those are best which we have

---

[97] Ps. 83:12 (RSV = Ps. 84:10).

not chosen, and which are less agreeable to us, or (to say better) those to which we have not much inclination, or (to speak frankly) those of our vocation and profession.

For example, this married woman would choose every sort of abjection rather than those of the married state; this religious would obey anybody but her superior; and you — you would much rather be chided by a superior in religion than by a father-in-law at home![98]

I say that to each one his own abjection is the best, and our choosing takes from us a great part of our virtues. Who will grant me the grace greatly to love our abjection, my dear child? Only He, who so loved His that He willed to die to preserve it. I have said enough. . . .

I can say no more to you concerning the apprehension you have of your troubles, nor the fear you have of impatiences in suffering them. Did I not say to you, the first time I spoke to you of your soul, that you applied your consideration too much to any trouble or temptation that may arise; that you must look at it only in a large way; that women, and men also, sometimes reflect too much on their troubles and that this entangles their thoughts, fears, and desires in one another, until the soul finds itself so knotted up that it cannot get free from them?

Do you remember Monsieur N., how his soul was entangled and mazed with vain fears at the end of Lent, and how hurtful it was to him? I beseech you for the honor of God, my child, do not be afraid of God, for He does not wish to do you any harm. Love Him strongly, for He wishes to do you much good.

[98] St. Francis is gently teasing Jane de Chantal with this remark about her father-in-law, with whom she lived and whose moods often caused her distress.

Thy Will Be Done

Walk quite simply in the shelter of our resolutions, and reject as cruel temptations the reflections that you make on your troubles.

What can I say to stop this flow of thoughts in your heart? Do not give way to anxiety about healing it, for this anxiety makes it worse. Do not force yourself to conquer your temptations, for these efforts will strengthen them. Despise them; do not occupy yourself with them. Represent to your imagination Jesus Christ crucified, in your arms and on your breast, and say a hundred times, kissing His side, "Here is my hope; here is the living fountain of my happiness; this is the heart of my soul, the soul of my heart. Never shall anything separate me from His love. I hold Him, and will not let Him go,[99] until He has put me in a state of safety." Say to Him very often, "What do I have upon earth, and what do I desire in Heaven, but You, O my Jesus?" "You are the God of my heart and my portion forever."[100]

Why do you fear, my child? Hear our Lord, who cries to Abraham, and to you also, "Fear not; I am thy helper."[101] What do you seek upon earth, save God? And you have Him. Remain firm in your resolutions. Keep yourself in the bark where I have placed you, and the storm may come. As Jesus lives, you shall not perish; He will sleep, but in time and place He will awaken to restore calm to you. St. Peter, says the Scripture, seeing the storm, which was very fierce, was afraid; and as soon as he became afraid, he began to sink and drown, at which he

---

[99] Song of Sol. 3:4.
[100] Ps. 72:25-26 (RSV = Ps. 73:25-26).
[101] Gen. 15:1.

cried, "O Lord, save me." And our Lord took him by the hand, and said to him, "Man of little faith, why didst thou doubt?"[102] Regard this holy Apostle. He walks dry-footed on the waters; the waves and the wind could not make him sink, but the fear of the wind and the waves makes him perish if his Master does not rescue him.

Fear is a greater evil than the evil itself. O daughter of little faith, what do you fear? No, fear not; you walk on the sea, amid the winds and the waves, but it is with Jesus. What is there to fear? But if fear seizes you, cry loudly, "O Lord, save me." He will give you His hand: clasp it tight, and go joyously on. To sum up, do not philosophize about your trouble, do not turn in upon yourself; go straight on. No, God cannot lose you, so long as you live in your resolution not to lose Him. Let the world turn upside down, let everything be in darkness, in smoke, in uproar — God is with us. And if God dwelleth in darkness and on Mount Sinai, all smoking and covered with the thunders, with lightnings and noises,[103] shall we not be well near Him?

Live, live, my dear child, live all in God, and fear not death, the good Jesus is all ours; let us be entirely His. Our most honored Lady, our Abbess, has given Him to us; let us keep Him well. Courage, my child. I am entirely

Yours, and more than yours,

Francis

---

[102]Matt. 14:24-31.
[103]Exod. 19:16, 18.

39

"Do not desire mortifications"

*To a woman striving
too hard for perfection*

Dear Madame,

. . . Without a doubt, we must resolve again and again to unite ourselves to God in order that we may keep such resolutions. But in your fervors, I do not want you to desire temptations or occasions for mortification. Since, by the grace of God they will not be lacking to you, there is no need to occupy your heart in desiring them. Instead you should occupy your heart in preparing and readying itself to receive them — not when you wish, but when God wishes to give them to you. . . .

But as for the complaint that you are miserable and unfortunate, my dear daughter, one must guard against this in every way. For beside the fact that such words are dishonorable for a servant of God, they come from a heart that is too dispirited and arise not so much from impatience as from anger.

Look here, my dear daughter, make a particular exercise of gentleness and acquiescence in the will of God, not only concerning extraordinary things, but chiefly in in these little daily irritations. Prepare yourself for it in the morning, after dinner, in saying grace before supper, after supper, and in the evening; and make it your standard practice for a time. But do these exercises with a tranquil and joyous spirit; and if distractions arise, humble yourself and start again.

It is a good thing to aspire in a general way to the highest perfection of the Christian life, but we do not need to know its nature in detail, except insofar as it concerns our improvement and advancement in daily affairs. From day to day, refer the progress of your general wish for perfection to the Providence of God; in this matter, cast yourself into His arms like a little child who, in order to grow, eats from day to day what his father gives to him, confident that his father will give to him in proportion to his appetite and his necessity.

Regarding your temptations to envy, practice what I advise in my book concerning these.[104] Because Holy Communion is profitable to you, receive it with spiritual fervor and a clear conscience. Live always joyously even amid your temptations. Do not do any other penance for the time being, and resolve yourself in a spirit of gentleness to bear lovingly with your neighbor, to visit the sick, and to have good courage. . . .

Good night, Madame, my very dear fellow godmother, my daughter. Your heart is God's; live happy in being so well accommodated. I am, with all my heart,

Your faithful servant and fellow godfather,

Francis

[104] *Introduction to the Devout Life*, Part 2, ch. 45, 52.

40

"Practice the mortifications that are given to you"

To a woman, on serving God
with gentleness and strength

Madame, my dearest sister,

It is impossible for me to restrain myself from writing to you at
all opportunities that present themselves. Do not worry yourself; no, believe me, practice serving our Lord with a gentleness full of strength and zeal. That is the true method of this
service. Wish not to do all, but only something, and without
doubt you will do much.

Practice the mortifications that most often present themselves to you; for this is the thing we must do first; after that
we will do others. Often kiss in spirit the crosses that our Lord
has Himself placed on your shoulders. Do not look whether
they are of a precious or fragrant wood; they are truer crosses
when they are of a wood that is vile, abject, and even stinking.
It is remarkable that this always comes back to my mind, and
that I know only this song. Without a doubt, my dear sister, it
is the canticle of the Lamb. This song is a little sad, but it is

harmonious and beautiful: "My father, be it not as I will but as Thou wilt."[105]

Magdalen seeks our Lord even though she is already holding Him; she demands Him from Himself. She does not see Him in the form in which she *wants* to see Him; this is why she is not content to see Him as He is, and seeks Him to find Him in some other guise. She wanted to see Him in His glorious dress, and not in a gardener's vile dress. But still at last she knew it was He, when He said "Mary."[106]

Look now, my dear sister, my child, it is our Lord in gardener's dress that you meet here and there every day in the occasions of ordinary mortifications that present themselves to you. You would like Him to offer you other and finer mortifications. Oh God, the finest are not the best. Do you not think He says "Mary, Mary"?

No, before you see Him in His glory, He wishes to plant in your garden many flowers, little and lowly, but to His liking; that is why He is dressed so.

May our hearts be ever united to His and our wills to His good pleasure. I am, without end and without measure, my dear sister,

Your most humble brother and servant,

Francis

---

[105]Matt. 26:39.
[106]John 20:14-16.

41

"O good Cross, so loved by my Savior!"

To a woman, on bearing the troubles of this life

My dearest daughter,

It is the truth that nothing is more capable of giving us a more profound tranquillity in this world than often to behold our Lord in all the afflictions that happened to Him from His birth to His death. We shall see there such a sea of contempt and insults, of poverty and indigence, of objections, of pains, of torments, of nakedness, of injuries, and of all sorts of bitterness, that in comparison with it we shall know that we are wrong when we call our little mishaps by the names of afflictions, pains, and contradictions; and we shall see that we are wrong in desiring patience for such trifles, since a single little drop of modesty is enough for bearing these things well.

I know exactly the state of your soul, and I seem to see it always before me, with all these little emotions of sadness, of surprise, and of disquiet that come troubling it. They trouble it because it has not yet laid deep enough in the will the foundations of abjection and of love of the Cross. My dearest daughter, a heart that greatly esteems and loves Jesus Christ crucified, loves His death, His pains, His torments, His being spat on, His insults, His destitutions, His hungers, His thirsts, His ignominies. And when some small share of these comes to it, it makes a very jubilee over them for joy, and embraces them amorously.

You must then every day, not during prayer, but at other times, when you are moving about, make a study of our Lord amid the pains of our redemption, and consider what a blessing it will be to you to share in them. You must try to discover the occasions in which you may gain this advantage — that is, in the contradictions you may perhaps meet in all your desires, but especially in those desires that seem to you the most just and lawful. And then, with a great love of the Cross and of the Passion of our Lord, you must cry out with St. Andrew, "O good Cross, so loved by my Savior, when will you receive me into your arms?"

Consider, my dearest child, that we are too delicate when we give the name "poverty" to a state in which we have not hunger, nor cold, nor ignominy, but simply some little contradiction to our desires. When we see one another again, remind me to speak to you a little about the tenderness and delicateness of your dear heart. For your peace and repose, you must be cured of this before all things; and you must form clearly in yourself the idea of eternity. Whoever thinks well on this troubles himself little about what happens in these three or four moments of mortal life.

Since you are able to fast half of Advent, you can continue to the end; I am quite willing for you to receive Communion two days together on feast days. You may certainly go to Mass after breakfast, only go with devotion. It is the old fashion of Christians. Our Lord does not regard these little things. Reverence is in the heart; you must not let your spirit feed on these little considerations.

Adieu, my dearest daughter. Hold me ever as all yours; for in truth I am so. God bless you. Amen.

Francis

42

"You only want to bear the crosses that you choose"

*To Jane de Chantal,
on true resignation of spirit*

Madame, my dearest sister,

May our glorious and holiest mistress and queen, the Virgin Mary, the feast of whose Presentation we celebrate today, present our hearts to her Son and give us His.

Your messenger reached me at the most troublesome and hardest place I can come across during the navigation that I make on the tempestuous sea of this diocese. It is incredible what consolation your letters brought me. . . . It is sufficiently said once for all: yes, God has given me to you, I say singularly, entirely, irrevocably. . . .

I come to your cross, and know not whether God has quite opened my eyes to see all its four ends. I profoundly desire and beg of Him that I may be able to say to you something thoroughly appropriate.

There is a certain powerlessness, you tell me, of the faculties or parts of your understanding, which hinders it from finding peace in the consideration of what is good. And what grieves you the most is that when you wish to form a resolution, you feel not your usual firmness, but encounter a certain barrier which brings you up short, and from this come the torments of temptations against the Faith. It is properly described, my dear daughter; you express yourself well. I am not sure whether I understand you properly.

You add that nevertheless your will, by the grace of God, intends nothing but simplicity and stability in the Church, and that you would willingly die for the Faith thereof. Oh, God be blessed, my dear child: "This sickness is not unto death, but that God may be glorified in it."[107]

"You have two nations in the womb" of your spirit, as was said to Rebecca. "The one fights against the other, but at last the younger will supplant the elder."[108] Self-love never dies until we die; it has a thousand ways of rooting itself in our soul. We cannot dislodge it; it is the eldest born of our soul, for it is natural, or, at least, connatural. It has a legion of soldiers with it, of movements, actions, and passions. It is cunning, and knows a thousand subtle turns.

On the other side, you have the love of God, which is conceived afterward, and is second born. It also has its movements, inclinations, passions, and actions.

These two children in one womb fight together like Esau and Jacob; whence Rebecca cried out, "Was it not better to die than to conceive with such pains?"[109] From these convulsions

[107]John 11:4.
[108]Gen. 25:23
[109]Gen. 25:22.

follows a certain disgust, which causes you to relish not the best meats. But what does it matter whether you do or do not relish, since you do not cease to eat well?

If I had to lose one of my senses, I would choose that it should be the taste, as it seems to me less necessary even than smell. Believe me, it is only taste that fails you, not sight. You see, but without satisfaction; you chew bread, but as if it were rope, without taste or relish. It seems to you that your resolutions are without force because they are not gay nor joyous. But you are mistaken, for the Apostle St. Paul very often had only that kind. . . .[110]

You do not feel yourself firm, constant, or very resolute. "There is something in me," you say, "which has never been satisfied; but I cannot say what it is." I should very much like to know what it is, my dear child, so I could tell it to you. But I hope that some day, hearing you at leisure, I shall discover it. Meanwhile, might it not be a multitude of desires which obstruct your spirit? I have been ill with that complaint. The bird fastened to the perch knows itself to be fastened and feels the shocks of its detention and restraint only when it wants to fly; and in the same way, before it has its wings, it knows its powerlessness only by the trial of flight.

For a remedy, then, my dear child, since you have not yet grown wings for flight and your own powerlessness hampers your efforts, do not flutter, do not make eager attempts to fly; have patience until you get your wings, like the doves. I greatly fear that you have a little too much ardor for the quarry, that you are overeager, and multiply desires a little too thickly. You

[110]Rom. 7:21-25.

see the beauty of illuminations, the sweetness of resolutions; you seem just about to grasp them; the proximity of good excites your appetite for it; and this other appetite agitates you and makes you dart forth, but for nothing. For the master keeps you fastened on the perch, or perhaps you have not your wings as yet; and meanwhile you grow thin by this constant movement of the heart, and continually lessen your strength. You must make trials, but moderate ones, without agitating yourself and without getting yourself overheated about them.

Examine well your practice in this matter; perhaps you will see that you let your spirit cling too much to desire for this sovereign sweetness that the sense of firmness, constancy, and resolution brings to the soul. You have firmness, for what else is firmness but to will rather to die than to sin or to quit the Faith? But you have not the sense of it; for if you had, you would have a thousand joys from it. So, then, check yourself; do not excite yourself; you will be all the better and your wings will thus strengthen themselves more easily.

Your eagerness, then, is a fault in you, and there is something (I do not know what) which is not satisfied; for this is a fault against resignation. You resign yourself well, but it is with a *but*; for you would very much like to have this or that, and you agitate yourself to get it.

A simple desire is not contrary to resignation, but this panting of heart, fluttering of wings, agitation of will, and multiplicity of dartings out — this, undoubtedly, is a fault against resignation. Courage, my dear sister: since our will belongs to God, doubtless we ourselves are His. You have all that is needed, but you have no sense of it; there is no great loss in that.

You cannot choose your cross

Do you know what you must do? You must be pleased not to fly, since you have not yet your wings. You make me think of Moses. That holy man, having arrived on Mount Pisgah, saw all the land of promise before his eyes, the land that for forty years he had aspired after and hoped for, amid the murmurs and seditions of his people, and amid the rigors of the deserts. He saw it and did not enter it, but died while looking at it.[111] He had your glass of water at his lips, and could not drink. Oh God, what sighs this soul must have fetched! He died there happier than many did in the land of promise, since God did him the honor of burying him Himself. And so, if you had to die without ever drinking the water of the Samaritan woman,[112] what would it matter, as long as your soul was received to drink eternally in the source and fountain of life? Do not excite yourself to vain desires, and do not even excite yourself about not exciting yourself; go quietly on your way, for it is good.

Know, my dear sister, that I write these things to you with much distraction, and that if you find them confused it is no wonder, for I am so myself, but (thank God) without disquiet. Do you want to know whether I speak the truth, when I say that there is in you a defect of entire resignation? You are quite willing to have a cross, but you want to choose it yourself; you would have it common, corporal, and of such and such a sort. What is that, my well-beloved daughter? Ah! no, I desire that your cross and mine be entirely crosses from Jesus Christ. And as to the imposition of them, and the choice, the good God

[111] Deut. 34:1-5.
[112] John 4:15.

163

knows what He does and why He does it: for our good, no doubt. Our Lord gave to David the choice of the rod with which he would be scourged; blessed be God for this.[113] But I think I would not have chosen; I would have let His divine majesty do all. The more a cross is from God, the more we should love it.

Well now, my sister, my daughter, my soul (and this is not too much, you well know), tell me, is not God better than man? Is not man a true nothing in comparison with God? And yet you have in me a man, or rather the merest nothing of all nothings, the flower of all misery, who loves no less the confidence that you have in him, although you may have lost the sense and taste of it, than if you had all the sentiments in the world. And will not God hold your good will agreeable, although without any feeling? "I am," said David, "like a bottle in the frost,"[114] which is of no use. Let there be as many drynesses, as much barrenness as you like, provided that we love God.

But, after all, you are not yet in the land in which there is no light, for you do have light sometimes, and God visits you. Is He not good, do you think? It seems to me this vicissitude makes you very agreeable to God. Still, I approve of your showing to our sweet Savior — but lovingly and without excitement — your affliction; and, as you say, He at least lets your soul find Him. For He is pleased that we should tell Him the pain He gives us, and lament to Him, provided it be lovingly and humbly and to Himself, as little children do when

[113]2 Kings 24:12-14 (RSV = 2 Sam. 24:12-14).
[114]Ps. 118:83 (RSV = Ps. 119:83).

their dear mother has spanked them. Meanwhile, there must be a little suffering, with sweetness. I do not think there is any harm in saying to our Lord, "Come into our souls." No, that has no appearance of evil. . . .

God wishes that I should serve Him in suffering dryness, anguish, and temptations, like Job, like St. Paul, and not in preaching.

Serve God as He wishes; you will see that one day He will do all you wish, and more than you know how to wish. . . .

Ah! Shall we not one day be all together in Heaven to bless God eternally? I hope so and rejoice in it.

The promise that you made to our Lord (never to refuse anything that someone asks you in His name) only obliges you to love Him properly. I fear that you might wrongly come to think that it obliges you to do things that would harm you [if they are asked in His name], such as giving more than you ought or giving indiscreetly. Your promise, then, has the understod condition that you will always observe true discretion, which is no more than to say that you will love God entirely, and will accommodate yourself to live, speak, act, and give according to His pleasure. . . .

I pray earnestly for our Celse-Bénigne, and all the little troop of girls.[115] I also recommend myself to their prayers. Remember to pray for my Geneva, that God may convert it.

Also remember to behave with a great respect and honor in all that regards the good spiritual father you know of; and again, when dealing with his disciples and spiritual children,

---

[115]St. Jane de Chantal had four children: her son Celse-Bénigne, and three daughters, Marie-Aimée, Françoise, and Charlotte.

let them acknowledge only true sweetness and humility in you. If you receive some reproaches, keep yourself gentle, humble, patient, and with no word save of true humility, for this is necessary. May God be forever your heart, your spirit, your repose; and I am, Madame,

Your very devoted servant in our Lord,

Francis

P.S. . . . I add, this morning, St. Cecilia's Day, that the proverb drawn from our St. Bernard, "Hell is full of good intentions," must not trouble you at all.[116] There are two sorts of good wills. The one says, "I would do well, but it gives me trouble, and I will not do it." The other, "I wish to do well, but I have not as much power as I have will; it is this which holds me back." The first fills Hell, the second Paradise. The first only begins to will and to desire, but it does not finish willing. Its desires have not enough courage; they are only abortions of will, and that is why it fills Hell. But the second produces entire and well-formed desires; it is for this that Daniel was called a "man of desires."[117] May our Lord deign to give us the perpetual assistance of His Holy Spirit, my well-beloved daughter and sister!

[116]St. Bernard of Clairvaux, *Soliloquies*, 1.
[117]Dan. 9:23.

Overcoming Fear, Temptation, Failure, and Discouragement

43

"We must be patient as we seek perfection"

*To a young woman who is
discouraged by spiritual failures*

Mademoiselle,

. . . My good daughter, as you have half got out of those terrible paths that you have had to travel, I think you should now take a little rest, and consider the vanity of the human spirit, how prone it is to entangle and embarrass itself within itself.

For I am sure you will note that those interior troubles you have suffered have been caused by a great multitude of consid-erations and desires produced by an intense eagerness to attain some imaginary perfection. I mean that your imagination had formed for you an ideal of absolute perfection, to which your will wished to lift itself; but frightened by this great difficulty — or rather impossibility — it remained in dangerous travail, unable to bring forth, to the great danger of the child. . . .

So now take a little breath, rest a little, and by considering the dangers escaped, avert those that might come afterward. Suspect all those desires that, according to the general opinion of good people, cannot come to effect: such as the desires for a certain Christian perfection that can be imagined but not practiced, in which many take lessons, but which no one realizes in action.

Know that the virtue of patience is the one that most assures us of perfection; and if we must have patience with others, so we must with ourselves. Those who aspire to the pure love of God have not so much need of patience with others as with themselves. We must suffer our imperfection in order to have perfection. I say suffer, not love or pet; humility feeds on this suffering.

The truth must be told: we are poor creatures, and can only just get on. But our God, who is infinitely good, is content with our little services and pleased with the "preparation of our heart."[118]

I will tell you what is meant by this preparation of heart. According to the Holy Scriptures, "God is greater than our heart,"[119] and our heart is greater than all the world. Now, when our heart, by itself, in its meditation prepares the service it will render to God — that is, when it makes its plans for serving God, honoring Him, serving our neighbor, mortifying the interior and exterior senses, and similar good resolutions — at such times it does wonders; it makes preparations and gets ready its actions for an eminent degree of admirable perfection. All this preparation is indeed in no way proportioned to the greatness of God Himself, who is infinitely greater than our heart; but still this preparation is generally

[118]Ps. 9:17 (RSV = Ps. 10:17).
[119]1 John 3:20.

greater than the world, than our strength, and than all of our exterior actions.

A soul that considers the greatness of God, His immense goodness and dignity, cannot satisfy herself in making great and marvelous preparations for Him. She prepares Him a flesh mortified beyond rebellion, an attention at prayer without distraction, a sweetness in conversation with no bitterness, a humility with no outbreak of vanity.

All this is very good; here are good preparations. And still more would be required to serve God according to our duty. But in the end of this we must find someone to do it: for when it comes to practice we stop short, and perceive that these perfections can neither be so grand in us nor so absolute. We can mortify the flesh, but not so perfectly that there shall be no rebellion; our attention will often be broken by distractions, and so on. And must we, for this, trouble, worry, and excite ourselves? Certainly not.

Are we to apply a host of desires to excite ourselves to arrive at this miracle of perfection? No. We may indeed make simple wishes that show our gratitude. I may say, "Ah! Why am I not as fervent as the Seraphim, in order better to serve and praise my God?" But I would not occupy myself with forming desires, as if I must in this world attain that exquisite perfection. I must not say, "I wish it; I will try to get it; and if I cannot reach it, I will be vexed."

I do not mean to say that we are not to put ourselves in that direction; but that we are not to desire to get there in one day, that is, in one day of this mortality. For this desire would torment us, and for nothing. To advance well we must apply ourselves to make good way in the road nearest to us, and to do the first day's journey. We must not busy ourselves with wanting to do the last, but remember that we are to do and work out the first.

I will give you this word, but you must keep it well: sometimes we occupy ourselves so much with being good angels that we neglect being good men and women. Our imperfection must accompany us to our coffin; we cannot walk without touching earth. We are not to lie or wallow there, but still we are not to think of flying. For we are but little chicks, and have not our wings yet. We are dying little by little, so we are to make our imperfections die with us day by day: dear imperfections, which make us acknowledge our misery and exercise us in humility, contempt of self, patience, and diligence, and in spite of which God regards the preparation of our hearts, which is perfect.

I know not if I am writing to the purpose, but it has come to my heart to say this to you, as I think that a part of your past trouble has come from this: that you have made great preparations, and then, seeing that the results were very small and that strength was insufficient to put in practice these desires, these plans, these ideas, you have had certain heartaches, impatiences, disquietudes, and troubles. Then followed distrusts, languors, depressions, or failings of heart. Well, if it is so, be wiser in the future.

Let us go by land, since the high seas make our heads turn, and give us retchings. Let us keep at our Lord's feet, with St. Mary Magdalen, whose feast we are celebrating. Let us practice certain little virtues proper for our littleness. Little pedlar, little pack. These are the virtues that are more exercised in going down, than in going up, and therefore they are suitable to our legs: patience, bearing with our neighbor, submission, humility, sweetness of temper, affability, toleration of our imperfection, and such little virtues as these. I am not saying that we should not try to mount by prayer, but that we should do so step by step.

I recommend to you holy simplicity: look before you, and regard not those dangers that you see far off. As you say, they seem to you armies, yet they are only willow branches; and while you are looking at them you may make some false step. Let us have a firm and general intention of serving God all our life, and with all our heart. Beyond that, let us have no solicitude for the morrow.[120] Let us only think of doing well today; when tomorrow arrives it will be called in its turn "today," and then we will think of it. We must here again have great confidence and acquiescence in the Providence of God. We must make provision of manna for each day and no more, and we must not doubt that God will send us more tomorrow, and after tomorrow, and all the days of our pilgrimage. . . .

Pray hard for me, I beg you. It is incredible how pressed down and oppressed I am by this great and difficult charge. This charity you owe me by the laws of our alliance, and I pay you back by the continual memory that I keep of you at the altar in my feeble prayers. Blessed be our Lord. I beg Him to be your heart, your soul, your life; and I am

Your servant,

Francis

[120]Matt. 6:34.

44

"Have courage, for you have only just begun"

To a young woman, on how to benefit from affliction

Mademoiselle,

I will gladly keep the copy of your vow, and God will keep the fulfilment of it. He was its author, and He will be its keeper. I will often make for this end St. Augustine's prayer: "Alas! Lord, here is a little chicken hidden under the wings of your grace. If it gets out of the shadow of its mother, the hawk will seize it. Let it then live by the help and protection of the grace that brought it forth."[121]

But look, my sister, you must not even think whether this resolution will be lasting; this must be held as so certain and settled that there can no longer be any doubt of it.

You do me a great favor in telling me a word about your inclinations. Regarding them I tell you that our affections, however slight they may be, injure our soul, when they are ill

---

[121] St. Augustine, *Confessions*, Bk. 12, ch. 27.

regulated. Keep them in check, and do not think them of small account; for they are of much weight in the scales of the sanctuary. . . .

So then, my good daughter, here you are afflicted, in just the proper way to serve God. Afflictions without abjection often puff the heart up instead of humbling it; but when we suffer evil without honor, or when contempt, abjection, and even dishonor are our evil, what occasions have we of exercising patience, humility, modesty, and sweetness of heart!

With a holy and glorious humility, St. Paul rejoiced that he and his companions were esteemed as the sweepings and rakings of the world.[122] You have still, you tell me, a very lively sense of injuries; but, my dear daughter, this word "still," to what does it refer? Have you already done much in conquering those enemies? I mean by this to remind you that we must have good courage and a good heart to do better in the future, since we are only beginning, even though we have a good desire to do well.

In order to become fervent in prayer, desire very much to be so, and willingly read the praises of prayer that are given in many books (for example, in Granada, the beginning of Bellintani, and elsewhere), because the appetite for food makes us very pleased to eat it.

You are very happy, my child, in having devoted yourself to God. Do you remember what St. Francis said when his father stripped him before the Bishop of Assisi: "Now, therefore, I can well say: 'Our Father, who art in Heaven.' "[123] David says,

[122] 1 Cor. 4:13.
[123] St. Bonaventure, *The Life of St. Francis*, ch. 2.

"My father and mother have left me, but the Lord has taken me up."[124] Make no apology for writing to me; there is no need, since I am so willingly devoted to your soul. May God bless it with His great blessings and make it all His! Amen.

Francis

---

[124]Ps. 26:10 (RSV = Ps. 27:10).

45

"Be gentle and charitable to your soul"

To a woman distressed by her sins

Madame,

I truly and greatly desire that when you think you can obtain any consolation by writing to me, you should do so with confidence.

We must join these two things together: an extreme affection for practicing our exercises very exactly — whether these concern prayer or virtues — and a calmness, quietness, and lack of dismay if we happen to commit a fault in them. For the practice of our exercises depends on our fidelity, which ought always to be entire, and grow from hour to hour; but faults come from our infirmity, which we can never put off during this mortal life.

My dearest daughter, when faults happen to us, let us examine our heart at once, and ask it if it has still alive and entire the resolution of serving God. I hope it will answer us *yes*, and that it would rather suffer a thousand deaths than withdraw itself from this resolution.

Thy Will Be Done

Then let us ask it, "Why then do you now fail; why are you so cowardly?" It will answer, "I have been surprised, I know not how; but I am now fallen, like this."

Well, my child, it must be forgiven; it is not by infidelity it falls; it is by infirmity. It needs then to be corrected, gently and calmly, and not to be vexed more and troubled. We ought to say to it: "Well now, my heart, my friend, in the name of God take courage; let us go on, let us beware of ourselves, let us lift ourselves up to our help and our God." Ah! My dear daughter, we must be charitable toward our soul, and not scold it, so long as we see that it does not offend out of set purpose.

You see, in this exercise we practice holy humility. What we do for our salvation is done for the service of God; for our Lord Himself has worked out in this world only our salvation. Do not desire the battle, but await it with firm foot. May our Lord be your strength. I am, in Him,

Your very affectionate servant,

Francis

46

"God loves greater infirmity with greater tenderness"

To a superior of the Visitation
nuns, on accepting imperfections

Madame,

It would have been to me a consolation beyond compare to see you all when I passed by, but since God did not will it, I could not will it. And meanwhile, my dearest daughter, I very willingly read your letters and answer them.

Our Blessed Lady knows, dearest child, that her Son thinks of you, and regards you with love! Yes, my dearest daughter, He thinks of you, and not only of you, but of the *least hair of your head*.[125] This is an article of faith, and we may not have the least doubt of it. But of course I know well you do not doubt it; you only express thus the aridity, dryness, and insensibility in which the lower portion of your soul finds itself now. "Indeed the Lord is in this place and I knew it not,"[126] said

---

[125]Matt. 10:30; Luke 21:18.
[126]Gen. 28:16.

Jacob — that is, I did not perceive it; I had no feeling of it; it seemed not so to me.

I have spoken of this in my *Treatise on the Love of God*, treating of the death of the soul and of resignations; I do not remember in which section.[127] And you can have no doubt about whether God regards you with love, for He regards lovingly the most horrible sinners in the world on the smallest true desire they have of conversion.

And tell me, my dearest child, have you not the intention of being God's? Do you not want to serve Him faithfully? And who gives you this desire and this intention, if not God Himself in His loving regard for you? The way is not to examine whether your heart pleases Him, but whether His heart pleases you. And if you look at His heart, it will be impossible for it not to please you, for it is a heart so gentle, so sweet, so condescending, so amorous of poor creatures if only they acknowledge their misery, so gracious toward the miserable, and so good to penitents! And who would not love this royal heart, paternally maternal toward us?

You say rightly, my dearest child, that these temptations come because your heart is without tenderness toward God. For it is true that if you had tenderness, you would have consolation; and if you had consolation you would no longer be in trouble. But, my daughter, the love of God does not consist in consolation, nor in tenderness; otherwise our Lord would not have loved His Father when He was "sorrowful unto death,"[128] and cried out, "My Father, my Father, why hast

[127]*Treatise on the Love of God*, Bk. 9, chs. 3, 11-13.
[128]Matt. 26:38.

Thou forsaken me?"[129] And it was exactly then that He made the greatest act of love it is possible to imagine.

In fact, we always wish to have a little consolation and sugar on our food — that is, we want to have the feeling of love and tenderness, and consequently consolation. And similarly, we greatly wish to be without imperfection. But, my dearest child, we must patiently continue to be of human nature and not angelic.

Our imperfections must not give us pleasure; indeed we should say with the holy Apostle, "Unhappy man that I am: who shall deliver me from the body of this death?"[130] But neither must they astonish us nor take away our courage. We must, indeed, draw from them submission, humility, and distrust of ourselves, but not discouragement, nor affliction of heart, much less distrust of the love of God toward us. So God does not love our imperfections and venial sins, but He loves us greatly in spite of them. Again, the weakness and infirmity of the child displeases the mother, yet she does not stop loving it, but even loves it tenderly and with compassion. In the same way, although God does not love our imperfections and venial sins, He does not cease to love us tenderly. Therefore, David had reason to say to our Lord, "Have mercy on me, O Lord, for I am weak."[131]

Well, now, that is enough, my dearest daughter.

Live joyously. Our Lord watches over you, and watches over you with love, and with greater tenderness insofar as you

---

[129]Cf. Matt. 27:46.
[130]Rom. 7:24.
[131]Ps. 6:3 (RSV = Ps. 6:2).

have more infirmity. Never let your spirit voluntarily nourish thoughts contrary to this; and when they come, do not regard them in themselves. Turn your eyes from their iniquity, and turn them back toward God with a courageous humility, to speak to Him of His ineffable goodness, with which He loves our failing, poor, and abject human nature, in spite of its infirmities.

Pray for my soul, my dearest child, and recommend me to your dear novices, all of whom I know, except Sister Colin.

I am entirely yours in our Lord. May He live for ever and ever in our hearts! Amen.

Francis

47

"We must bear ourselves until God bears us to Heaven"

To a woman struggling with spiritual problems

Madame,

Your letter of January 2 has given me an extreme satisfaction, because in the midst of the miseries that you describe to me, I note (I think) some progress and profit that you have made in the spiritual life. I shall be briefer in answering you than I could wish, because I have less leisure and more hindrance than I expected. I will, however, say quite enough for this time, awaiting another chance of writing to you at full length.

You say that you are afflicted because you do not reveal yourself to me perfectly enough, as you think. And I say to you that although I do not know what you do in my absence, for I am no prophet, I think all the same, that in spite of the little time I have seen and heard you, it is not possible to know your inclinations and their sources better than I do. . . . However little you open to me the door of your spirit, I seem to see in quite openly. It is a great advantage for you, since you wish to use me for your salvation.

Thy Will Be Done

You complain that many imperfections and defects occur in your life, in opposition to the desire you have for the perfection and purity of love for our God. I answer you that we cannot quit ourselves altogether while we are here on earth; we must always bear ourselves until God bears us to Heaven; and as long as we bear ourselves we shall bear nothing of any worth. So we must have patience, and not expect to be able to cure in a day so many bad habits, which we have contracted by the little care we have had of our spiritual health.

God has cured some souls suddenly, without leaving any trace of their former maladies, as He did in the case of Magdalen, who in an instant from a sewer of the water of corruption was changed into a spring of the water of perfections, and was never muddied from that moment.

But also has this same God left in some of His dear disciples many marks of their bad inclinations for some time after their conversion, and all for their greater profit. Witness the blessed St. Peter, who after his first calling stumbled several times into imperfections, and once fell down altogether, and very miserably, by his denial.

Solomon says that the handmaid who suddenly becomes mistress is a very insolent animal.[132] There would be great danger that the soul that had long served its own passions might become proud and vain, if in a moment she became entirely mistress of them. It is necessary that little by little and foot by foot we obtain this dominion, which has cost the saints many decades of years. The soul needs, if you please, to have patience with all the world, but first with itself.

[132]Prov. 30:23.

You do nothing, you say, in prayer. But what would you do, except what you do, which is to present and represent to God your nothingness and your misery? Beggars harangue us best when they expose to our sight their ulcers and needs.

But sometimes again you do nothing of all this, as you tell me, but remain there like a phantom or a statue. Well, and that is not a little thing. In the palaces of princes and kings, statues are put that are only of use to gratify the prince's eyes. Be satisfied, then, with serving for that purpose in the presence of God; He will give life to this statue when He likes.

The trees only fructify through the presence of the sun — some sooner, others later, some every year, others every three years, and not always equally. Let us be very happy to be able to stay in the presence of God, and let us be satisfied that He will make us bear our fruit, sooner or later, always or sometimes, according to His good pleasure, to which we must entirely resign ourselves.

The word that you said to me contains wonders: "Let God put me in what sauce He likes, provided that I serve Him." But take care to masticate it again and again in your spirit; make it melt in your mouth and do not swallow it in a lump. St. Teresa of Avila, whom you so love (for which I am glad), says somewhere that very often we say such words by habit, and with a slight attention.[133] We think we say them from the bottom of our soul, but it is not so at all, as we discover afterward in practice.

Well! You say that in whatever sauce God puts you, it is all one. Now you know well in what sauce He has put you, in

---

[133]St. Teresa of Avila, *The Way of Perfection*, ch. 38.

what state and condition; and tell me, is it all one? You know also that He wants you to satisfy this daily obligation of which you write to me, and yet it is not all one to you. My God! How subtly self-love insinuates itself into our affections, however devout they seem and appear.

This is the grand truth: we must look at what God wants, and when we know it we must try to do it joyfully or at least courageously. And not only that, but we must love this will of God, and the obligation that comes from it, were it that we must keep pigs all our life and do the most abject things in the world. For in what sauce God puts us, it should be all one. It is the bull's-eye of perfection at which all of us must aim; and he who gets nearest gets the prize.

But courage, I beseech you. Accustom your will little by little to follow that of God, wherever He leads you. Make your will very sensitive to the voice of conscience saying, "God wills it"; and little by little these repugnances that you feel so strongly will grow weaker, and soon will cease altogether. But particularly you ought to struggle to hinder the exterior manifestations of the interior repugnance you have, or at least to make them gentler. Among those who are angry or discontented some show their displeasure only by saying "My God, what is this?" And others say words that show more irritation and not only a simple discontent, but a certain pride and spleen. What I mean to say is that we must little by little amend these demonstrations, making them less every day.

As to the desire you have to see your friends very far advanced in the service of God and the desire of Christian perfection, I praise it infinitely; and as you wish, I will add my weak prayers to the supplications you make about it to God.

But, Madame, I must tell you the truth; I ever fear in such desires that are not of the essence of our salvation and perfection, that there may mingle some suspicion of self-love and our own will. For instance, I fear that we may so much occupy ourselves in these desires that are not necessary to us, as not to leave room enough in our soul for desires that are more necessary and useful, as of our own humility, resignation, sweetness of heart, and the like. Or again I fear that we may have so much ardor in these desires as to make them bring us disquiet and eagerness, or finally, I fear that we may not submit them so perfectly to the will of God as is expedient.

Such things do I fear in such desires. For this reason, I pray you to take good care of yourself that you fall not into them, as also I pray you to pursue this desire quietly and sweetly, that is, without importuning those whom you want to persuade to this perfection, and even without showing your desire. For, believe me, this would impede the affair instead of advancing it. You must then by example and words sow among them very quietly the things that may induce them to your design, and, without making appearance of wishing to instruct or gain them, you must throw little by little holy inspirations and thoughts into their minds. Thus will you gain much more than in any other way, above all if you add prayer. . . .

Francis

48

"Self-love can be mortified, but never dies"

*To a nun, on the
masks that self-love wears*

My dearest child,

Oh! Would to God that it was the treatise of heavenly love that kept me occupied all the morning![134] It would soon be finished, and I should be very happy to apply my soul to such sweet consideration. But it is the infinite number of little follies that the world necessarily brings me every day that causes me trouble and annoyance, and makes my hours useless. Still, so far as I can run away from these troubles, I ever keep writing a few more lines about this holy love, which is the bond of our mutual love.

Well, let us come to your letter. Self-love can be mortified in us, but still it never dies; indeed, from time to time and on different occasions, it produces shoots in us, which show that, although cut off, it is not rooted out. This is why we have not

[134]*Treatise on the Love of God.*

the consolation that we ought to have when we see others do well. For what we do not see in ourselves is not so agreeable to us; and what we do see in ourselves is very sweet to us, because we love ourselves tenderly and amorously. But if we had true charity, which makes us have one same heart and one same soul with our neighbor, we should be perfectly filled with consolation when our neighbor did well.

This same self-love makes us willing enough to do things of our own choice, but not by the choice of another, or by obedience; we would do it as coming from us, but not as coming from another. It is always we ourselves who seek our own will and our own self-love; on the contrary, if we had the perfection of the love of God, we should prefer to do what was commanded because it comes more from God, and less from ourselves.

As for taking more pleasure in doing difficult things ourselves than in seeing them done by others, this may either be through charity or because self-love secretly fears that others may equal or surpass us. By goodness of disposition we are sometimes more distressed to see others ill treated than ourselves; sometimes, however, our distress arises because we think ourselves braver than they, and believe that we should support the trouble better than they, according to the good opinion we have of ourselves.

The proof of this is that ordinarily we would rather have small troubles than let another have them; but great troubles we wish more for others than ourselves. Without doubt, my dear child, the repugnance we have to the supposed exaltation of others comes from this, that we have a self-love that tells us we should do even better than they, and that the idea of our good designs promises us wonders from ourselves, and not so much from others.

Besides all this, know, my very dear child, that the things you feel are only the dispositions of the lower part of your soul; for I am sure that the superior part disavows it all. It is the only remedy we have: to disavow the dispositions, invoking obedience, and protesting that we love it, in spite of all repugnance, more than our own choice, praising God for the good which one sees in others, and beseeching Him to continue it. And so we must do with other ill-feelings.

We must be in no way surprised to find self-love in us, for it never leaves us. Like a fox it sleeps sometimes, then all of a sudden leaps on the chickens; for which reason we must constantly keep watch on it, and patiently and very quietly defend ourselves from it. But if sometimes it wounds us, we are healed by unsaying what it has made us say and disavowing what it has made us do. . . .

God bless you, my dear child.

Francis

49

"We must attain holy indifference"

*To a woman, on
struggling against self-love*

Madame,

God, our Savior, knows well that among the affections He has placed in my soul, that of cherishing you extremely and honoring you most perfectly, is one of the strongest, and entirely invariable, exempt from change and from forgetfulness. Well now, since this protestation has been made very religiously, I will say this little word of liberty and candor, and will begin again to call you by the cordial name of "my dearest daughter," since in truth I feel that I am cordially your father by affection.

My dearest daughter, then, I have not written to you; but tell me, I pray, have you written to me since my return into this country? No? Even so, you have not forgotten me. Surely, neither have I forgotten you; for I say to you with all fidelity and certainty that what God wants me to be to you, that I am; I quite feel that I shall be such forever, most constantly and most thoroughly, and I have in this a singular satisfaction, which is accompanied by a great deal of consolation and profit for my soul.

I was waiting for you to write, not from thinking you *should* write, but never doubting that you *would*; then I could write more at large. But if *you* had waited longer, believe me, my very dear daughter, *I* could not have, any more than I could ever leave out your very dear self and all your dear family in the offering that I make daily to God the Father on the altar, where you hold, in the commemoration that I make of the living, quite a special rank; and indeed you are quite especially dear to me.

Oh! I see, my dearest child, in your letter, a great reason to bless God for your soul, which keeps holy indifference *in fact*, although not *in feelings*. My dearest child, all this you tell me of your little faults is nothing. These little surprises of the passions are inevitable in this mortal life. On this account does the holy Apostle cry to Heaven: "Alas! Miserable man that I am! I perceive two men in me, the old and the new; two laws, the law of the flesh, and the law of the spirit; two operations, nature and grace. Ah! Who shall deliver me from the body of this death?"[135]

My daughter, self-love dies only with our body; we must always feel its open attacks or its secret attempts while we are in this exile. It is enough that we do not consent with a willed, deliberate, fixed, and entertained consent. And this virtue of indifference is so excellent that our old man, in the sensible part, and human nature according to its natural faculties, is not capable of it. As a child of Adam (although exempt from

[135]Rom. 7:21-24.

all sin and all the appearances thereof), even our Lord was, in His sensible part and His human faculties, by no means indifferent, but desired not to die on the Cross. The indifference was all reserved, with its exercise, to the spirit, to the superior portion, to the faculties inflamed by grace, and in general to Himself as the new man.

So then, remain in peace. When we happen to break the laws of indifference in indifferent things, or by the sudden sallies of self-love and our passions, let us at once, as soon as we can, prostrate our heart before God, and say, in a spirit of confidence and humility, "Have mercy on me, O Lord, for I am weak."[136] Let us arise in peace and tranquillity, knot again the thread of our indifference, and then continue our work. We must not break the strings nor throw up the lute when we find a discord; we must bend our ear to find whence the disorder comes, and gently tighten or relax the string as the evil requires.

Be in peace, my dearest child, and write to me in confidence when you think it will be for your consolation. I will answer faithfully and with a particular pleasure, your soul being dear to me, like my own.

We have had these past eight days our good Monsignor de Belley, who has favored us with his visit and has given us excellent sermons. Guess if we have often spoken of you and yours! But what joy when Monsieur Jantet told me that my dearest little godson was so nice, so gentle, so handsome, and even already in some sense so devout. I assure you, in truth, my dearest daughter, that I feel this with an incomparable love,

[136]Ps. 6:3 (RSV = Ps. 6:2).

and I recollect the grace and sweet little look with which he received, as with infantile respect, the sonship of our Lord from my hands. If I am heard, he will be a saint, this dear little Francis; he will be the consolation of his father and mother, and will have so many sacred favors from God, that he will obtain me pardon of my sins, if I live until he can love me actually. In short, my dearest daughter, I am very perfectly and without any condition or exception,

Your very humble and very faithful brother,
companion, and servant,

Francis

50

"Lean on the mercy of God"

To a woman wondering
whether she has done her duty

My dearest daughter,

I received your two letters and see clearly that all the trouble you have had is truly nothing more than a spiritual encumbrance that has come from two desires that have not been satisfied in you: one, the desire to serve God in the situation that presents itself to you; the other, the desire to know whether you have faithfully done your duty. And in the one and the other you have suffered a distress that has troubled and disquieted you, and has finally weighed you down.

Well, without a doubt you have done your duty well. Your spirit, which always tends a bit toward indignation, lets you discern little of what you have done; and the same spirit, greatly desiring to fulfil its obligation and not being able to convince itself that it has done it, has fallen into sadness and discouragement or disgust.

Well, my dear daughter, know that you must in this case cheer yourself up, forget all that, and humble yourself before our Lord. Remember that your sex and your vocation only allows you to stop the evil that takes place outside of your home by your good inspirations and intentions, by simple, humble, and loving reproaches when someone has committed a wrong, and by notification of the authorities when that is possible — I will talk about that another time.

To this I add, as general advice, that when we cannot discern whether we have done our duty well in some matter and are in doubt about whether we have offended God, we must then humble ourselves, ask God to forgive us, request more light for another time, and then forget all about what has happened and get back to our ordinary business. A curious and anxious search to determine whether we have acted well comes undoubtedly from the self-love that makes us want to know whether we are brave — just at that point where pure love of God tells us: "Whether you were truant or coward, humble yourself, lean upon the mercy of God, always ask for pardon, and with a renewed confession of fidelity, go back to the pursuit of your perfection."

. . . May God be always our only love and goal, my dearest daughter, and I am in Him entirely

Yours,

Francis

51

"To change the world, we must change ourselves"

*To a woman angered by
sinfulness in the world*

Madame,

No doubt you would explain yourself much better and more freely by speaking than by writing; but, while waiting for God to will it, we must use the means which offer themselves. You see, lethargies, languors, and numbness of the senses cannot be without some sort of sensible sadness, but so long as your will and the substance of your spirit is quite resolved to be all to God, there is nothing to fear, for these are natural imperfections, and rather maladies than sins or spiritual faults. Still you must stir yourself up and excite yourself to courage and spiritual activity as far as possible.

Oh! Death is terrible, my dear daughter, it is very true, but the life which is beyond, and which the mercy of God will give us, is also very desirable indeed; and so we must by no means fall into distrust. Although we are miserable, we are not nearly so much so as God is merciful to those who want to love Him and who have placed their hopes in Him. When the blessed Cardinal Borromeo was on the point of death, he had the image of our dead Savior brought to him, in order to sweeten his death by that of his Savior. It is the best of all remedies against the fear of our death, this thought of Him who is our life: you must never think of the one without adding the thought of the other.

My God! Dear daughter, do not examine whether what you do is little or much, good or ill, provided it is not sin, and provided that in good faith you will to do it for God. As much as you can, do perfectly what you do, but when it is done, think of it no more; go simply along the way of our Savior, and do not torment your spirit.

We must hate our faults, but with a tranquil and quiet hate, not with an angry and restless hate; and so we must have patience when we see them, and draw from them the profit of a holy abasement of ourselves. Without this, my child, your imperfections, which you scrutinize so subtly, will trouble you by getting still more subtle, and by this means sustain themselves, as there is nothing that more preserves our weeds than disquietude and eagerness in removing them. . . .

To be dissatisfied and fret about the world when we must of necessity be in it, is a great temptation. God's Providence is wiser than we. We fancy that by changing our ships, we shall get on better; *yes, if we change ourselves.*

My God, I am sworn enemy of these useless, dangerous, and bad desires; for although what we desire is good, the desire is bad, because God does not will us this sort of good, but another, in which He wants us to exercise ourselves. God wishes to speak to us in the thorns and the bush, as He did to

Moses;[137] and we want Him to speak in the small wind, gentle and fresh, as He did to Elijah.[138] May His goodness preserve you, my daughter; but be constant, courageous, and rejoice that He gives you the will to be all His. I am, in this goodness, entirely

Yours,

Francis

---

[137]Exod. 3:2.
[138]3 Kings 19:12 (RSV = 1 Kings 19:12).

52

"In patience shall you possess your soul"

*To Jane de Chantal, on
patience and bearing temptations*

Madame,

. . . I praise God for the constancy with which you bear your tribulations. I still see in it, however, some little disquiet and eagerness, which hinders the final effect of your patience. "In your patience," said the Son of God, "you shall possess your souls."[139] To possess fully our souls is then the effect of patience; and in proportion as patience is perfect, the possession of the soul becomes more entire and excellent. Now, patience is more perfect as it is less mixed with disquiet and eagerness. May God then deign to deliver you from these two troubles, and soon afterward you will be free altogether.

Good courage, I beseech you, my dear sister. You have only suffered the fatigue of the road three years, and you crave repose. But remember two things. The first one is that the

[139]Luke 21:19.

children of Israel were forty years in the desert before arriving in the country of rest that was promised them, and yet six weeks might easily have sufficed for all this journey. But it was not lawful to inquire why God made them take so many turns, and led them by ways so rough, and all those who murmured died before their arrival.[140] The other thing is that Moses, who was the greatest friend of God in all that multitude, died on the borders of the land of repose, seeing it with his eyes, and not able to have the enjoyment of it.[141]

Oh, might it please God that we should little regard the course of the way we tread, and have our eyes fixed on Him who conducts us, and on the blessed country to which it leads! What should it matter to us whether it is by the deserts or by the meadows we go, if God is with us and we go into Paradise? Trust me, I pray you, *cheat* your trouble all you can: if you feel it, at least do not look at it, for the sight will give you more fear of it than the feeling will give you pain. For just this reason the eyes of those who are going to suffer some painful application of the iron are covered. I think you dwell a little too much on the consideration of your trouble.

And as for what you say, that it is a great burden to will and to be unable, I will not say to you that we must only will what we can achieve, but I do say it is a great power before God to be able to will. Go further, I beg you, and think of that great dereliction which our Master suffered in the Garden of Olives and see how this dear Son, having asked consolation from His good Father, and knowing that He willed not to give it Him,

[140]Num. 14:36-37.
[141]Deut. 34:4-5.

thinks of it no more, strives after it no more, seeks it no more; but, as if He had never thought of it, executes valiantly and courageously the work of our redemption.

After you have prayed to the Father to console you, if it does not please Him to do it, think of it no more, and stiffen your courage to work out your salvation on the Cross, as if you were never to descend from it, and as if you would never more see the sky of your life clear and serene.

What do you want? You must see and speak to God amid the thunders and the whirlwinds. You must see Him in the bush and amid the thorns; and to do this, the truth is that we must take off our shoes, and make a great abnegation of our wills and affections. But the divine goodness has not called you to the state in which you find yourself without strengthening you for all this. It is for Him to perfect His work. True, it takes quite a while, because the matter requires it; but patience.

In short, for the honor of God, acquiesce entirely in His will, and by no means believe that you can better serve Him otherwise; for He is never well served save when He is served as He wills.

Now He wants you to serve Him without relish, without sentiment, with repugnances and convulsions of spirit. This service gives you no satisfaction, but it contents Him. It is not to your pleasure, but it is to His.

Suppose you were never to be delivered from your troubles, what would you do? You would say to God, "I am Yours; if my miseries are agreeable to You, increase their number and duration." I have confidence in God that you would say this, and think no more of them; at least you would no longer excite yourself. Do the same about them now, and grow familiar with your burden, as if you and it were always to live together. You will find that when you are no longer thinking of deliverance, God will think of it; and when you are no longer disquieted, God will be there. . . .

Courage, I beseech you; let nothing move you. It is still night, but the day approaches; yes, it will not delay. But, meantime, let us put in practice the saying of David: "Lift up your hands to the holy places in the night, and bless the Lord."[142] Let us bless Him with all our heart, and pray Him to be our guide, our bark, and our port.

I do not intend to answer your last letter in detail, save in certain points which seem to me more pressing.

You cannot believe, my dearest child, that temptations against the Faith and the Church come from God. But who ever told you that God was the author of such things? [God permits] much darkness, much powerlessness, much being tied to the perch, much dereliction and loss of vigor, much disorder of the spiritual stomach, and much bitterness in the interior mouth (which makes bitter the sweetest wine in the world) — but suggestions of blasphemy, infidelity, disbelief? Oh no, they cannot come from our good God; His bosom is too pure to conceive such objects.

Do you know how God acts in this? He allows the evil maker of such wares to come and offer them for sale, so that by our contempt of them we may give witness to our affection for divine things. And for this, my dear sister, my dearest child, are we to become disquieted, are we to change our attitude?

[142]Ps. 133:2 (RSV = Ps. 134:2).

Oh God, no, no! It is the Devil who goes all around our soul, raging and fuming, to see if he can find some gate open. He did so with Job, with St. Anthony, with St. Catherine of Siena, and with an infinity of good souls that I know, and with mine, which is good for nothing, and which I know not. And for what? For all this, my good daughter, must we grow troubled? Let the Devil rage; keep all the entrances closely shut. He will tire at last, or if he does not tire, God will compel him to lift the siege.

Remember what I told you once before. It is a good sign when the Devil makes so much noise and tempest round about the will; it is a sign that he is not within. And courage, my dear soul; I say this word with great feeling and in Jesus Christ. My dear soul, courage, I say. So long as we can say with resolution, even if without feeling, *Vive Jésus!*, we must not fear.

And do not tell me that you say this with cowardice, without force or courage, but as if by a violence that you do yourself. Oh God! There it is then, the holy violence that bears Heaven away.[143]

Look, my child, this is a sign that all is taken, that the enemy has gained everything in our fortress except the keep, which is impregnable, unseizable, and which cannot be ruined except by itself. Finally, it is free will that, quite naked before God, resides in the supreme and most spiritual part of the soul, that depends on no other than its God and itself. When all the other faculties of the soul are lost and subject to the enemy, free will alone remains mistress of itself so as not to give its consent.

[143]Matt. 11:12.

Thy Will Be Done

Now, do you see souls afflicted because the enemy, occupying all the other faculties, makes in them his clamor and most extreme hubbub? Scarcely can one bear what is said and done in this superior will. The superior will has indeed a voice more clear and telling than that of the inferior will; but this latter has a voice so harsh and so noisy that it drowns out the clearness of the other.

Lastly, note this: while a temptation displeases you there is nothing to fear; for why does it displease you, save because you do not will it? In a word, these burdensome temptations come from the malice of the Devil; but the pain and suffering that we feel come from the mercy of God who, against the will of the enemy, draws from his malice holy tribulation, by which He refines the gold that He would put into His treasures.

I sum up my remarks in this way: your temptations are from the Devil and from Hell, but your pains and afflictions are from God and Paradise. The mothers are from Babylon, but the daughters from Jerusalem. Despise the temptations; embrace the tribulations.

I will tell you one day when I have plenty of leisure, what evil it is that causes these obstructions of spirit; it cannot be written in a few words.

Have no fear, I beg you, of giving me trouble; for I protest that it is an extreme consolation to be pressed to do you any service. Write to me then, and often, and without order, and in the most simple way you can; I shall always have an extreme contentment in it.

I am going in an hour to the little hamlet where I am to preach, God willing to employ me both in suffering and in preaching. May His name be forever blessed! . . .

In patience you possess your soul

You cannot have too much confidence in me, who am perfectly and irrevocably yours in Jesus Christ, whose dearest graces and benedictions I wish you a thousand and a thousand times a day. Let us live in Him and for Him. Amen.

Your most assured and very devoted
servant in our Lord,

Francis

53

"Do not worry yourself about temptations"

To Jane de Chantal,
on dealing with temptations

My child,

You will have now at hand, I am sure, the three letters that I have written to you, and which you had not yet received when you wrote to me on the tenth of August. It remains for me to answer yours of the tenth, since by the preceding I have answered all the others.

Your temptations against the Faith have come back, and although you do not respond to them even with a single word, they press you. You do not respond to them: that is good, my child. But you think too much of them; you fear them too much; you dread them too much. They would do you no harm without that. You are too sensitive to temptations. You love the Faith, and would not have a single thought come to you contrary to it; and as soon as a single one arises, you grieve about it and distress yourself. You are too jealous of this purity of faith; everything seems to spoil it. No, no, my child, let the wind blow, and think not that the rustling of the leaves is the clashing of arms.

Lately I was near the beehives, and some of the bees flew onto my face. I wanted to raise my hand, and brush them off. "No," said a peasant to me, "do not be afraid, and do not touch them. They will not sting you at all; if you touch them they will bite you." I trusted him; not one bit me. Trust me; do not fear these temptations. Do not touch them; they will not hurt you. Pass on, and do not occupy yourself with them. . . .

Today is St. Augustine's feast day; you may guess whether I have entreated for you both the Lord, and the servant and the mother of the servant of God.[144] How my soul loves yours! Let your soul continue to confide in mine and love it well. God wishes it, my dearest child, I know it well, and He will be glorified by it. May God be our heart, my child; and I am in Him and by His will, all yours. Live joyful, and be generous. God, whom we love, and to whom we are vowed, wishes us to be such. It is He who has given me to you: may He be for ever blessed and praised!

Francis

P.S. I was closing this letter, badly done as it is, and here are brought to me two others, one of the sixteenth, the other of the twentieth of August, enclosed in a single packet. I see nothing in them save what I have said; you fear temptations too much. There is no harm but that. Be quite convinced that all the temptations of Hell cannot stain a soul that does not

[144]St. Monica.

love them: let them have their course then. The Apostle St. Paul suffered terrible ones, and God did not will to take them from him, and all this occurred out of love.

Come, come, my child, courage; let the heart be ever with its Jesus; and let this vile beast bark at the gate as much as he likes. Live, my dear child with the sweet Jesus and your holy Abbess amid the darkness, the nails, the thorns, the spears, the derelictions; and with your mistress St. Monica, live long in tears without gaining anything. At last, God will raise you up, and will cause you to rejoice, and "will make you see the desire of your heart."[145]

I hope so; and if He does not do this, still we will not cease serving Him. And for that reason He will not cease to be our God, for the affection we owe Him is of an immortal and imperishable nature.

Francis

---

[145]Cf. Ps. 20:3 (RSV = Ps. 21:2).

54

"We must not be fearful of fear"

*To a man fearful
of judgment after death*

Sir,

I am truly in great distress to know how much you have suffered in this severe and painful illness, from which, I hope, you will recover. I should have had very much more pain if on every hand I had not been assured that, thanks to God, you have been in no sort of danger, and that you have begun to recover your strength, and are in the way of health again.

But what gives me more apprehension now is that besides the evil you suffer through corporal infirmities, you are overcome by a violent melancholy. For I know how much this will retard the return of your health, and indeed will work in the opposite direction.

It is here, sir, that my heart is greatly oppressed; and because of the greatness of the lively and extreme affection with which it cherishes you (beyond what can be said), it has an extraordinary compassion for yours. If you please, sir, tell me,

Thy Will Be Done

I beg you, what reason have you for nourishing this sad humor that is so injurious to you? I fancy that your mind is still encumbered with some fear of sudden death and of the judgments of God. Alas! What a dreadful torment is this! My soul, which endured it for six weeks, is very capable of feeling compassion for those who are afflicted with it.

But, sir, I must speak a little with you, heart to heart, and tell you that whoever has a true desire both to serve our Lord and to avoid sin, ought not at all to disquiet himself with the thought of death or of the divine judgments. Although both of these are to be feared, still the fear should not be of that terrible and terrifying kind that beats down and depresses the vigor and strength of the soul, but should be a fear so mixed with confidence in the goodness of God that by this means it becomes gentle.

And we should not, sir, doubt whether we may trust in God when we find it difficult to keep from sin, or when we imagine or fear that in occasions and temptations we may not be able to resist. Oh no, sir; for distrust of our strength is not a failure of resolution, but a true acknowledgment of our misery. It is a better state of mind to distrust our own power of resistance to temptation than to consider ourselves as sufficiently strong and safe.

Only we must take care that what we *do not* expect from our strength, we *do* expect from the grace of God. Hence many, with great consolation, have promised themselves to do wonders for God, but, when it came to the point, have failed. And many who have had great distrust of their strength and great fear of failing on trial, when the time came have suddenly done wonders, because this great sense of their weakness has urged them to seek the aid and succor of God, to watch, to pray, and to humble themselves, so that they may not enter into temptation.

I say that if we feel we have neither strength nor even any courage to resist temptation if it presented itself at once to us (provided that we still desire to resist it and we hope that if it came, God would help us), and if we ask His help, we must by no means distress ourselves, since it is not necessary for us always to feel strength and courage. It suffices that we hope and desire to have it at the time and place. It is not necessary to feel in ourselves any sign or any mark that we shall have this courage; it is enough that we hope that God will help us.

Samson, who was called "the strong," never felt the supernatural strength with which God helped him except at the actual times; and hence it is said that when he met the lions or the enemies, the spirit of God came upon him to kill them.[146] So God, who does nothing in vain, does not give us strength or courage when there is no need to use them; but at the necessary time nothing is wanting. Hence we must always hope that in all occurrences He will help us, if we call upon Him. And we should always use the words of David, "Why are you sorrowful, my soul, and why do you disquiet me? Hope in the Lord,"[147] and his prayer, "When my strength fails, O Lord, forsake me not."[148]

Well, then, since you desire to be entirely God's, why do you fear your weakness, in which you are not to put any sort of

[146]Judg. 14:6, 19; 15:14.
[147]Ps. 41:6 (RSV = Ps. 42:5).
[148]Ps. 70:9 (RSV = Ps. 71:9).

trust? Do you not hope in God? Ah! "He who trusteth in Him, shall he ever be confounded?"[149] No, sir, he shall never be. I beseech you, sir, to quell all the objections that might arise in your mind. You need make no other answer to them save that you desire to be faithful on all occasions, and that you hope God will make you so. There is no need to test your spirit, to see whether it would or no. These tests are illusive; many souls are valiant while they do not see the enemy, who are not valiant in his presence; and, on the contrary, many fear before battle, to whom the actual danger gives courage. We must not fear fear.

So much on this point, sir. Meanwhile, God knows what I would do and suffer to see you entirely delivered. I am

Your very humble and affectionate servant,

Francis

---

[149]Cf. Ecclus. 2:11 (RSV = Sirach 2:10).

55

"Constrain yourself only to serving God well"

To Jane de Chantal,
on calming the troubled spirit

My dear child,

At last I write to you, by Monsieur Favre, and still without full leisure, for I have had to write many letters, and although you are the last to whom I write, I have no fear of forgetting. I was sorry the other day to have written you so many things on this trouble of mind that you had. For since it was nothing in real truth, and since when you had communicated it to Father Gentil, it all vanished, I had only to say "*Deo Gratias.*" But, you see, my soul is liable to outpourings with you, and with all those whom I love.

Oh God! My child, what good your hurts do me! For then I pray with more attention, I put myself before our Lord with more purity of intention, I place myself more wholly in indifference. But, believe me, either I am the most deluded man in the world or our resolutions are both from God and unto His greater glory.

Thy Will Be Done

No, my child, look not either to left or right; and I do not mean do not look at all, but do not look so as to occupy yourself, to examine anxiously, to hamper and entangle your spirit in considerations from which you can find no outlet. For if, after so much time, after so many petitions to God, we cannot decide without difficulty, how can we expect by considerations, some coming without any reflection, others arising from simple feelings and taste — how can we expect, I say, to decide well?

So then, let us leave that alone, let us speak of it no more. Let us speak of a general rule that I want to give you: it is that in all I say to you, you must not be too particular. All is meant in a large sense, for I would not have you constrain your spirit to anything, save to serve God well, and not to abandon but to love your resolutions. As for me, I so love mine that whatever I see seems to me insufficient to take away an ounce of the esteem I have of them, even though I see and consider others more excellent and more exalted.

Ah! My dear child, that also is an entanglement about which you write to me via Monsieur de Sauzea. This dreadful din . . . Oh God, my child, when it happens to you, can you not prostrate yourself before God and say to Him quite simply, "Yes, Lord, if you will it, I will it; and if you wish it not, I wish it not," and then pass on to some little exercise or act that may serve as a distraction?

But, my child, what you do instead is this: when this trifling matter presents itself, your mind is grieved, and does not want to look at it. It fears that this may check it; this fear draws away the strength of your mind, and leaves the poor thing faint, sad, and trembling. This fear displeases it, and brings forth another fear lest this first fear, and the fright that it gives, be the cause of the evil; and so you entangle yourself. You fear the fear; then you fear the fear of fear. You are vexed at the vexation, and then you are vexed for being vexed at the vexation. So I have seen many, who, having got angry, are afterward angry for getting angry. And all this is like the rings that are made in water, when a stone is thrown in: a little circle is formed, and this forms a greater, and this last another.

What remedy is there, my dear child? After the grace of God, the remedy is not to be so delicate. Consider (here is another outpouring of my spirit, but there is no help for it): those who cannot suffer the itching of an insect and expect to get rid of it by dint of scratching, flay their hands. Laugh at the greater part of these troubles; do not stop to think about throwing them off; laugh at them; turn away to some action; try to sleep well. Imagine (I mean to say, think) that you are a little St. John, who is going to sleep; and rest on the bosom of our Lord, in the arms of His Providence.

And courage, my child. We have no desire except for the glory of God, is that not so? No, no, at least certainly not any known desire; for if we knew it, we would instantly tear it from our heart. And so, what do we torment ourselves about? *Vive Jésus!* I think sometimes, my child, that we are filled with Jesus; at least we have no deliberate contrary will. It is not in a spirit of arrogance I say this, my child; it is in a spirit of trust and to encourage ourselves. . . .

I find it is nine o'clock at night; I must have my supper, and I must say the Office so as to be able to preach at eight tomorrow, but I seem to be unable to tear myself away from this paper.

Thy Will Be Done

And now I must tell you, in addition, this little folly; it is that I preach much to my liking in this place. I say something, I scarcely know what it is, which these good people understand so well that they would willingly almost answer me.

Adieu, my child, my dearest child. I am, without compare,

Yours,

Francis

56

"True simplicity is always good and agreeable to God"

To Jane de Chantal,
on charity and humility

My dear, my very dear child,

I have been ten entire weeks without having a bit of news of you, and your last letters were at the beginning of last November. But the chief thing is that my fine patience almost disappeared from my heart, and I think would have disappeared altogether, if I had not remembered that I must keep it so that I may preach it to others. But at last, my dearest child, yesterday comes a packet, like a fleet from the Indies, rich in letters and spiritual songs.

Oh! How welcome it was, and how I cherished it! There was one of the twenty-second of November, another of the thirtieth of December, and the third of the first of January of this year. But if all the letters I have written you during this time were in one packet, they would be in far greater number, for as far as possible I have always written, both by Lyons and by Dijon. Let this be said to discharge my conscience, which would hold itself forever guilty, were it not to respond to the heart of a daughter so uniquely loved. I am going to tell you many things in a desultory fashion, according to the subject of your letters. . . .

We must, after the example of our St. Bernard, be quite clean and neat, but not particular or dainty. True simplicity is always good and agreeable to God. I see that all the seasons of the year meet in your soul, that sometimes you feel the winter; on the morrow drynesses, distractions, disgust, troubles, and wearinesses; sometimes the dews of May, with the perfume of holy flowers; sometimes the ardors of desire to please our good God. There remains only autumn, of whose fruit, as you say, you do not see much.

Still it often happens that in threshing the corn, and pressing the grapes, there is found more than the harvest or vintage promised. You would like all to be spring and summer; but no, my dear child, there must be change in the interior, as well as in the exterior. It is in Heaven that all will be spring with respect to beauty, autumn with respect to enjoyment, and summer with respect to love. There will be no winter in Heaven, but here winter is needed for abnegation and a thousand little virtues that are exercised in time of sterility.

Let us always walk our little step; if we have a good and resolute affection, we can never go otherwise than well. No, my dearest child, the exercise of virtues does not require that we should ever keep actually attentive to all. That would certainly too much entangle and hamper our thoughts and affections. Humility and charity are the mainstays; all the others are attached to them. We need only to keep ourselves well in these two virtues: one the lowest, the other the highest, since the preservation of the whole edifice depends on the foundation and the roof. When one keeps the heart bound to the exercise of these, there is no great difficulty in getting the others. These are the mothers of the virtues, which follow them as little chickens follow their mother hens.

Oh! Indeed I greatly approve of your being schoolmistress. God will be pleased, for He loves little children, and as I said at catechism the other day (to induce our ladies to take care of the girls) the angels of little children love with a special love those who bring up children in the fear of God, and who instill into their tender hearts true devotion, just as, on the contrary, our Lord threatens those who scandalize children with the vengeance of their angels. . . .[150]

What more shall I tell you? I have just come from giving catechism where we have had a bit of merriment with our children, making the congregation laugh a little by mocking balls and costume parties, for I was in my best humor, and a great audience encouraged me with its applause to play the child with the children. They tell me it suits me well, and I believe it.

May God make me a true child in innocence and simplicity; but am I not also a true simpleton to say that to you? I can't help it; I make you see my heart as it is, and in the variety of its movements, that, as the Apostle says, you may think no more of me than is in me.[151]

Live joyful and courageous, my dear child. You must have no doubt that Jesus Christ is ours. "Yes," a little girl once said

[150]Matt. 18:6, 10.
[151]2 Cor. 12:6.

to me, "He is more mine than I am His, and more mine than I am my own."

I am going to take Him for a little while into my arms, this sweet Jesus, to carry Him in the procession of the Confraternity of the Cord,[152] and I will say to Him the *Nunc Dimittis*, with Simeon.[153] For, truly, if He is with me, I care not where I go. I will speak to Him of your heart, and believe me, with all my power, I will beg Him to make you His very dear and well-beloved servant. Ah! My God! How am I indebted to this Savior, who so loves us, and how would I, once for all, press and glue Him to my breast.

I mean to yours, as well, since He has willed that we should be so inseparably one in Him. *Adieu*, my most cherished, and truly most dear sister and daughter.

May Jesus ever be in our hearts; may He live and reign there eternally; may His holy name, and that of His glorious Mother, be ever blessed! Amen. *Vive Jésus*, and let the world die if it does not wish to live for Jesus. Amen.

Francis

[152]See above, note 3.
[153]Luke 2:29-32.

57

"We must do all by love
and nothing by force"

*To Jane de Chantal, on
temptation and spiritual liberty*

Madame,

May God give me power equal to the will that I have to make myself clearly understood in this letter! I am sure that I should give you consolation about part of what you want to know from me, and particularly in the doubts that the enemy suggests to you on the choice you have made of me as your spiritual father. I will do what I can to express in a few words what I think is necessary for you on this subject. . . .

Know that, as I have just said, from the beginning of your conferring with me about your interior, God gave me a great love of your soul. When you opened yourself to me more particularly, it was an obligation on my soul to cherish yours more and more, which made me write to you that God had given me to you. I do not believe that anything could be added to the affection I felt in my soul, and above all when praying to God for you.

But now, my dear child, a certain new quality has developed that I seem unable to name. I can only say its effect is a great interior sweetness that I feel in wishing you the perfection of the love of God, and other spiritual benedictions. No, I do not add a single line to the truth. I speak before the "God of my heart"[154] and yours: every affection has its particular difference from others; the affection that I have for you has a special quality which immensely consoles me, and which, to sum up, is extremely profitable to me. Hold that for the truest truth, and doubt it no more. I did not mean to say so much, but one word brings on another, and besides I think you will apply it properly. . . .

You ask me for remedies in the trouble caused you by the wicked one's temptations against the Faith and the Church; at least so I understand you. I will say what God gives me to say.

In this temptation you must behave as in temptations of the flesh, disputing neither little nor much. Do as the children of Israel did with the bones of the Paschal lamb, which they did not even try to break, but simply threw into the fire.[155] You must not reply at all, nor appear to hear what the enemy says. Let him clamor as he likes at the door; you must not say as much as "Who goes there?"

"True," you will tell me, "but he worries me, and his noise makes those within unable to hear one another speak." It is all the same. Have patience — we must prostrate ourselves before God, and remain there at His feet. He will understand by this humble behavior that you are His, and that you want His help,

[154]Ps. 72:26 (RSV = Ps. 73:26).
[155]Exod. 12:10.

although you cannot even speak. But above all keep yourself well shut in, and do not open the door at all, either to see who it is or to drive the nuisance away. At last he will get tired of crying out, and will leave you in peace. "And never too soon," you will say.

I ask that you obtain a book called *On Tribulation,* composed by Father Ribadaneira, in Spanish, and translated into French.[156] The Father Rector will tell you where it is printed; read it carefully.

Courage, then; it will come to an end at last. Provided the Devil enter not, it matters not. And meanwhile it is an excellent sign when the enemy beats and blusters at the door; for it is a sign that he does not have what he wants. If he had it, he would not cry out any more; he would enter and stay. Take note of this, so as not to fall into scruples.

After this remedy, I give you another. Temptations against the Faith go straight to the understanding, to make it parley and think and dream about them. Do you know what you must do while the enemy is occupied trying to scale the intellect? Sally out by the gate of the will, and make a good attack against him.

That is, when a temptation against the Faith comes to engage you ("How can this be?" "But what if this . . . ?" "But what if that . . . ?"), instead of disputing with the enemy by argument, let your affective part rush forth vehemently upon him, and even joining the exterior voice to the interior, cry: "Ah, traitor! Ah, wretch! Thou hast left the Church of the

---

[156]Pedro de Ribadenaira (1526-1611), Spanish Jesuit, historian, and ascetical writer.

angels, and wishest me to leave the Church of the saints! Disloyal, faithless, perfidious one, thou didst present to the first woman the apple of perdition, and now thou wantest me to eat of it! 'Get thee behind me, Satan! It is written: thou shalt not tempt the Lord thy God.'[157] No, I will not reason or dispute. Eve wishing to dispute with the Devil was seduced and ruined. *Vive Jésus,* in whom I believe! *Vive* the Church, to which I cling!" And similar words of fire.

You must also say words to Jesus Christ, and to the Holy Spirit (such as He will suggest to you), and even to the Church: "O mother of the children of God, never will I let myself be separated from you; I will to live and to die in your holy bosom."

I know not if I make myself understood. I mean to say that we must fight back with affections and not with reasons, with passions of the heart and not with considerations of the mind. It is true that in these times of temptation the poor will is quite dry, but so much the better. Its acts will be so much the more terrible to the enemy, who, seeing that instead of retarding your progress he gives you an opportunity of exercising a thousand virtuous affections, and particularly the protestation of faith, will leave you at last. . . .

Finally, these temptations are only afflictions like others; and we must place our reliance on the saying of the Holy Scripture: "Blessed is he that suffers temptation; for when he has been tried he shall receive the crown of glory."[158] Know that I have seen few persons make progress without this trial,

[157]Matt. 4:10, 7.
[158]James 1:12.

and we must have patience. Our God, after the storms, will send the calm. . . .

Every day take a good half-hour's spiritual reading; this is quite enough for each day. On feasts you can assist at Vespers, and say the office of our Lady. But if you have a great taste for the prayers you have been used to saying, do not change, I beg. And if you happen to omit something that I order, do not make a scruple of it; for here is the general rule of our obedience written in great letters: "We must do all by love, and nothing by force; we must love obedience rather than fear disobedience."

I leave you the spirit of liberty: not that which excludes obedience — for this is the liberty of the flesh — but that which excludes constraint, scruple, and worry. If you very much love obedience and submission, I wish that if some just or charitable necessity requires you to omit your spiritual exercises, you do so, letting this omission be a type of obedience, and compensated for by love. . . .

About the spirit of liberty, I will tell you what it is.

Every good man is free from acts of mortal sin, and does not keep any affection for it. This is a liberty necessary for salvation. I do not speak of this.

The liberty of which I speak is the liberty of well-beloved children. And what is it? It is a detachment of the Christian heart from all things in order to follow the known will of God. You will easily understand what I mean to say if God gives me now the grace to propose to you the marks, signs, effects, and occasions of this liberty.

We ask from God before all things, that His name may be hallowed, His kingdom come, and His will be done on earth as it is in Heaven. All this is no other thing than the spirit of liberty. For provided that the name of God is sanctified, that His majesty reigns in you, and that His will is done, then the soul cares for nothing else.

The first mark of this spirit of liberty: the soul which has this liberty is not attached to consolations, but receives afflictions with all the sweetness that the flesh can permit. I do not say that it does not love and desire consolations, but I say that it does not attach its heart to them.

The second mark of this spirit of liberty: it does not at all attach its affection to spiritual exercises, so that, if by sickness or other accident it is kept from them, it feels no grief at it. Here also I do not say it does not love them, but I say it is not attached to them.

Such a heart scarcely loses its joyfulness, because no privation makes him sad whose heart is quite unattached. I do not say he does not lose joyfulness, but that he scarcely loses it then — that is, only for a short time.

The effects of this liberty are a great suavity of soul, a great gentleness and condescension in all that is not sin or danger of sin, a temper sweetly pliable to the acts of every virtue and charity. For example, if you interrupt a soul that is attached to the exercise of meditation, you will see it leave with annoyance, worried and surprised. A soul that has true liberty will leave its exercise with an equal countenance, and a heart gracious toward the importunate person who has inconvenienced her. For it is all one to her whether she serves God by meditating or serves Him by bearing with her neighbor: both are the will of God, but the bearing with her neighbor is necessary at that time.

The occasions of this liberty are all the things that happen against our inclination, for whoever is not attached to his inclinations is not impatient when they are contradicted.

This liberty has two opposite vices, instability and constraint, or dissolution and slavery. Instability, or dissolution of spirit, is a certain excess of liberty, by which we change our exercises, our state of life, without proof or knowledge that such change is God's will. On the smallest occasion, practices, plan, and rule are changed. For every little occurrence we leave our rule and laudable custom, and thus the heart is dissipated and ruined, and is like an orchard open on all sides, whose fruits are not for its owners, but for all passersby.

Constraint or slavery is a certain want of liberty by which the soul is overwhelmed with either disgust or anger when it cannot do what it has planned, although still able to do better. For example, I plan to make my meditation every day during the morning. If I have the spirit of instability or dissolution, on the least occasion in the world I shall put it off until the evening — for a dog that kept me from sleeping, for a letter I have to write, of no urgency at all. On the other hand, if I have the spirit of constraint or servitude, I shall not leave my meditation at that hour even if a sick person has great need of my help at the time, even if I have a dispatch that is of great importance and which cannot well be put off, and so on.

It remains for me to give you one or two examples of this liberty that will better make you understand what I cannot properly describe. But first I must tell you that you are to observe two rules to avoid stumbling in this point.

A person should never omit his exercises and the common rules of the virtues unless he sees the will of God on the other side. Now, the will of God shows itself in two ways, by necessity and charity. I want to preach this Lent in a small corner of my diocese. If, however, I get ill or break my leg, I must not be grieved or disquieted because I cannot preach; for it is certainly the will of God that I should serve Him by suffering and not by preaching. Or if I am not ill, but an occasion presents itself of going to some other place, where, if I do not go, the people will become Huguenots[159] — there is the will of God sufficiently declared to turn me gently from my design.

The second rule is that when we are to use liberty for the sake of charity, it must be without scandal and without injustice. For example, I may know that I could be more useful somewhere very far from my diocese. I cannot use liberty in this, for I would scandalize and commit injustice by leaving, since I am obliged to be here. Likewise, it would be a false liberty for married women to separate themselves from their husbands without a legitimate reason, under the pretext of devotion and charity. Hence, this liberty never interferes with vocations; on the contrary, it makes each one satisfied with his own vocation, since each should know that he is placed in it by the will of God.

Now, I want you to look at Cardinal Borromeo, who is going to be canonized in a few days.[160] His spirit was the most exact, rigid, and austere that it is possible to imagine. He drank nothing but water and ate nothing but bread; he was so austere that, after he was archbishop, he only entered twice during twenty-four years into the house of his brothers, when ill, and

[159]Calvinist French Protestants.

[160]See above, note 61.

only twice into his garden. Yet, this rigorous soul, when eating with the Swiss, his neighbors, as he often did to keep a good influence over them, made no difficulty in drinking toasts with them at each meal, besides what he drank for his thirst. There is a trait of holy liberty in the most austere man of this age. A dissolute spirit would have done too much; a constrained spirit would have considered it a mortal sin; a person with the spirit of liberty would have done it for charity.

Spiridion, an ancient bishop,[161] having received a pilgrim almost dead with hunger during Lent, and in a place in which there was nothing but salted meat, had some of this cooked and offered it to the pilgrim. The pilgrim was unwilling to take it in spite of his great necessity. Spiridion had no need of it, but ate some first for charity, in order to remove by his example the scruple of the pilgrim. Here was a charitable liberty in this holy man.

Father Ignatius of Loyola,[162] who is going to be canonized, ate meat on Wednesday in Holy Week on the simple order of the doctor, who judged it expedient for a little sickness he had. A spirit of constraint would have had to be begged to do so for three days.

But I want now to show you a shining sun of detachment, a spirit truly free and unbound by any engagement, holding only to the will of God. I have often wondered what was the greatest mortification of all the saints I know, and after many considerations I have found this: St. John the Baptist went

---

[161] St. Spiridion (died c. 348), bishop of Tremithus in Cyprus.

[162] St. Ignatius Loyola (c. 1495-1556), founder of the Society of Jesus, otherwise known as the Jesuits.

into the desert at the age of five years, knowing that our and his Savior was born quite near him — one day's journey, or two or three, or so.

God knows whether St. John's heart, touched with the love of his Savior from the womb of his mother Elizabeth, desired to enjoy His holy presence. Yet St. John stayed twenty-five years there in the desert, without going even once to see our Savior. Then he remains elsewhere to catechize, without going to our Lord, and waits for Him to come. Afterward, having baptized our Lord, he does not follow Him, but stays to do his own work.

Oh God! What a mortification of spirit! To be so near his Savior, and not to see Him! To have Him so near and not to enjoy Him! And what is this but to have the heart free from all, even from God Himself, to do the will of God and to serve Him? To leave God *for* God, and not to love God, in order so much the better and more purely to love Him! This example overwhelms my soul with its grandeur.

I forgot to say that the will of God is known not only by necessity and charity, but by obedience, so that he who receives a command must believe that it is the will of God for him to obey it.

Am I not writing too much? But my spirit runs quicker than I wish, carried on by the ardent desire of serving you. . . .

Remember the day of blessed King St. Louis, the day on which you took again the crown of your kingdom from your own soul to lay it at the feet of the King Jesus; the day on which you renewed your youth, like the eagle,[163] plunging it

---

[163] Ps. 102:5 (RSV = Ps. 103:5).

in the sea of penance; a day, which is the harbinger of the eternal day of your soul.

Remember that after you pronounced your grand resolutions declaring yourself to be all God's — body and heart and soul — I said "Amen" on behalf of the whole Church our Mother; and at the same time, the Holy Virgin with all the saints and the blessed made their great "Amen" and "Alleluia" resound in Heaven.

Remember to hold that all the past is nothing, and that every day you must say with David, "Now I have begun" to love my God properly.[164] Do much for God, and do nothing without love. Apply all to this love; eat and drink for it.

Be devout to St. Louis, and admire in him his great constancy. He was king at twelve, had nine children, and made war continually against either rebels or the enemies of the Faith. He was king more than forty years and at the end of them all, his confessor, a holy man, swore that having confessed him all his life, he had never found that he had fallen into mortal sin. He made two voyages beyond the sea; in both he lost his army, and in the latter he died of pestilence, after having for a long time visited, helped, served, dressed, and cured the plague-stricken of his army — and he died joyous, constant, with a verse of David in his mouth.[165]

I give you this saint as your special patron for all the year; have him before your eyes, with the others named above. In the coming year, if it please God, I will give you another, after you have profited well in the school of this one. . . .

[164]Ps. 76:11 (verse missing from RSV).
[165]"I will enter into your house, O Lord" (Ps. 5:8; RSV = Ps. 5:8).

Thy Will Be Done

If I decide for myself, I shall never finish this letter, which is written without other intention than to answer yours. Still I must finish it, begging the great assistance of your prayers, and declaring my great need of them. I never pray without mentioning you in part of my supplications. I never salute my angels without saluting yours; do the same for me, and get Celse-Bénigne to do it. I always pray for him and for all your household! Be sure that I never forget them, nor their deceased father, your husband, in holy Mass.

May God be your heart, your mind, your soul, my dearest sister; and I am in His merciful love,

Your very devoted servant,

Francis

58

"Be then all for God"

———————

*To a young woman, on
giving oneself to God*

My dearest daughter,

I say to you with all my heart, *Adieu*.[166] May you ever be "for God" in this mortal life, serving Him faithfully in the pain of carrying the Cross after Him here and in the heavenly life, blessing Him eternally with all the heavenly court. It is the great good of our souls to be "for God," and the greatest good to be only "for God."

He who is only "for God" is never sorrowful, except for having offended God; and his sorrow for that dwells in a deep but tranquil and peaceful humility and submission. Then he raises himself up in the divine goodness, by a sweet and perfect confidence, without annoyance or bitterness.

He who is "for God" only, seeks Him only; and because God is not less in adversity than prosperity, such a one remains

———

[166]This letter is framed around a play on words. In French the word for *goodbye is Adieu*, which literally means "for God" (*à* = for; *Dieu* = God).

at peace in adversity. He who is "for God" only, often thinks of Him amidst all the occupations of this life. He who is "for God" only, wishes everyone to know whom he serves, and tries to take the means proper for remaining united to Him.

Be then completely "for God," my dearest daughter, and be only His, only wishing to please Him, and His creatures in Him, according to Him, and for Him. What greater blessing can I wish you? Thus, then, by this desire, which I will unceasingly make for your soul, my dearest daughter, I say to you *Adieu;* and praying that you often recommend me to His mercy, I remain

Your most humble servant,

Francis

Biographical Note

St. Francis de Sales

1567-1622

Doctor of the Church and patron saint of writers, St. Francis de Sales was remarkable "not only for the sublime holiness of life which he achieved, but also for the wisdom with which he directed souls in the ways of sanctity."[167]

The eldest of thirteen children, Francis de Sales was born in 1567 to a noble family in the French-speaking Duchy of Savoy (an area straddling present-day eastern France and western Switzerland). He received a superb education in both France and Italy. Although intended by his father for a diplomatic career, St. Francis was ordained to the priesthood in the diocese of Geneva in 1593. Shortly thereafter, he was sent to the Chablais region of the Savoy on a mission to persuade those who had fallen under Calvinist influence to return to the practice of Catholicism. St. Francis spent four years laboring at this difficult task, during which he suffered many indignities. More than once he was thrown out of his lodgings, and had to sleep in the open air. Many times he celebrated Mass in

[167]Pope Pius XI, *Rerum omnium perturbationem*, 4.

empty churches or continued preaching while the congregation walked out. Nevertheless, St. Francis's unflagging poise and kindness in this mission led to its eventual success. By the turn of the century, the majority of the area's inhabitants had returned to the Catholic faith.[168]

After his election as bishop of Geneva in 1602, St. Francis continued his apostolic efforts to win souls back to the Catholic Church. At the same time, St. Francis sought to build a broad community of devout persons within the Church who would live the life of Christian perfection in all their varied states and vocations.[169]

It was St. Francis's absolute conviction that "holiness is perfectly possible in every state and condition of secular life," whether one is male or female, rich or poor, single or married.[170] He expounded this view at length in his classic work *The Introduction to the Devout Life*. This conviction permeates the advice he gave to the many persons from all walks of life to whom he gave spiritual direction, both in person and in letters renowned for their spiritual wisdom, their psychological insight, their graciousness, and what one scholar has called their "inspired common sense."[171]

Jane Frances Frémyot, Baroness de Chantal, is the most famous of those who came to St. Francis for spiritual direction.

[168]Ibid., 8.

[169]*Francis de Sales, Jane de Chantal: Letters of Spiritual Direction*, ed. Wendy M. Wright and Joseph F. Power (New York: Paulist Press, 1988), 23.

[170]Pius XI, *Rerum omnium perturbationem*, 13.

[171]Elisabeth Stopp, ed., *St. Francis de Sales: Selected Letters* (New York: Harper and Bros., 1960), 33-34.

An aristocratic young widow with four children, she met St. Francis in 1604. In cooperation with her, St. Francis founded the Visitation of Holy Mary in Annecy in Savoy, a congregation for unmarried and widowed women who aspired to religious life but who were not sufficiently young, healthy, or free of family ties to enter one of the more austere women's orders of the day. The Visitation eventually developed into a cloistered religious order devoted to prayer and the cultivation of the "little virtues" St. Francis praised so highly. The order flourished during St. Francis's lifetime and afterward. St. Jane de Chantal was herself canonized in 1751.

After nearly thirty years of tireless labor on behalf of the Church and its members, St. Francis de Sales died of a cerebral hemorrhage in Lyons, France, on December 28, 1622. He had been travelling in the entourage of the king and queen of France at the time, but rather than stay in royal quarters, he lodged in the gardener's cottage on the grounds of the Visitation convent in that city. Fittingly for this apostle of the little virtues, he died in that modest cottage.

St. Francis de Sales was canonized in 1665. His feast day is celebrated on January 29.

Source of the Letters

Source of the Letters
of Saint Francis de Sales

*The French originals of the letters in this
collection can be found in the Oeuvres de Saint
François de Sales, Édition Complète, vols. 11-21
(Annecy: J. Niérat, 1900-1923)*

1. "Thy will be done"
   Letter 483 to Mademoiselle Clément, October 1608

2. "Do the will of God joyfully"
   Letter 233 to Madame Brulart, October 13, 1604

3. "Serve God where you are"
   Letter 480 to Etienne Dunant, priest of Gex, September 25, 1608

4. "Let us be what we are, and let us be it well"
   Letter 289 to Madame Brulart, June 10, 1605

5. "Our faith should be naked and simple"
   Letter 1854 to Sister de Blonay, November 28, 1621

6. "There are two principal reasons for prayer"
   Letter 441 to Mademoiselle de Soulfour, 1605-1608

7. "Little virtues prepare for contemplation of God"
   Letter 505 (in fragmentary form) to Jane de Chantal, 1605-1608

Thy Will Be Done

8. "We must remain in the presence of God"
    Letter 838 to Jane de Chantal, 1611-1612

9. "Never does God leave us save to hold us better"
    Letter 308 to Jane de Chantal, September 8, 1605

10. "Marriage is an exercise in mortification"
    Letter 1998 to an unnamed young woman, undated

11. "As far as possible, make your devotion attractive"
    Letter 217 to Madame Brulart, May 3, 1604

12. "Have patience with everyone, including yourself"
    Letter 455 to Madame de la Fléchère, May 19, 1608

13. "Keep yourself gentle amid household troubles"
    Letter 518 to Madame Brulart, mid-March 1609

14. "Do what you see can be done with love"
    Letter 1254 to Madame Guillet de Monthoux,
    November 10, 1616

15. "Parents can demand more than God Himself"
    Letter 1778 to the Countess de Dalet, April 25, 1621

16. "Avoid making your devotion troublesome"
    Letter 367 to Madame Brulart, late October 1606

17. "Have contempt for contempt"
    Letter 1988 to an unnamed young woman, undated

18. "Lord, what would You have me do?"
    Letter 1971 to an unnamed man of Dijon, undated

19. "Take Jesus as your patron"
    Letter 637 to Celse-Bénigne de Chantal, son of Jane de Chantal,
    December 8, 1610

20. "Remain innocent among the hissings of serpents"
    Letter 1539 to Madame de Villesavin, July or August 1619

21. "Never speak evil of your neighbor"
    Letter 508 (in fragmentary form) to Jane de Chantal, 1605-1608

Source of the letters

22. "Extravagant recreations may be blameworthy"
    Letter 1668 to Madame de Granieu, June 16 or 20, 1620

23. "We must not ask of ourselves what we don't have"
    Letter 1704 to an unnamed woman, September 29, 1620

24. "If you get tired kneeling, sit down"
    Letter 469 to Madame de la Fléchère, July 16, 1608

25. "You will not lack mortifications"
    Letter 1289 to Madame de Grandmaison, late March 1617

26. "We must always walk faithfully"
    Letter 1861 to a woman of Grenoble, December 13, 1621

27. "Illness can make you agreeable to God"
    Letter 477 to an unnamed woman, possibly a nun, September 9, 1608

28. "You are being crowned with His crown of thorns"
    Letter 738 to an unnamed woman, 1610-1611

29. "Often the world calls evil what is good"
    Letter 1713 to Madame de Granieu, October 23, 1620

30. "Rest in the arms of Providence"
    Letter 870 to Jane de Chantal (possibly regarding one of her "spiritual" children), April or May 1613

31. "In confidence, lift up your heart to our Redeemer"
    Letter 1295 to Madame de Veyssilieu, April 7, 1617

32. "We must slowly withdraw from the world"
    Letter 230 to President Bénigne Frémyot, father of Jane de Chantal, October 7, 1604

33. "This dear child was more God's than yours"
    Letter 2034 to Baron Prosper de Rochefort, January 20, 1614

34. "Think of no other place than Paradise or Purgatory"
    Letter 1089 to Madame de Peyzieu, mid-June 1615

35. "How tenderly I loved her!"
    Letter 418 to Jane de Chantal, November 2, 1607

Thy Will Be Done

50. "Lean on the mercy of God"
    Letter 517 to Madame de la Fléchère, March 1609

51. "To change the world, we must change ourselves"
    Letter 512 to Madame de la Fléchère, January 20, 1609

52. "In patience shall you possess your soul"
    Letter 273 to Jane de Chantal, February 18, 1605

53. "Do not worry yourself about temptations"
    Letter 306 to Jane de Chantal, August 28, 1605

54. "We must not be fearful of fear"
    Letter 1974 to an unnamed man, undated

55. "Constrain yourself only to serving God well"
    Letter 436 to Jane de Chantal, March 7, 1608

56. "True simplicity is always good and agreeable to God"
    Letter 385 to Jane de Chantal, February 11, 1607

57. "We must do all by love and nothing by force"
    Letter 234 to Jane de Chantal, October 14, 1604

58. "Be then all for God"
    *Letter 1548 to an unnamed young woman of Paris,
    September 7, 1619*

SOPHIA INSTITUTE PRESS

Sophia Institute is a non-profit institution that seeks to restore man's knowledge of eternal truth, including man's knowlege of his own nature, his relation to other persons, and his relation to God.

Sophia Institute Press serves this end in a number of ways. It publishes translations of foreign works to make them accessible for the first time to English-speaking readers. It brings back into print many books that have long been out-of-print. And it publishes important new books that fulfill the ideals of Sophia Institute. These books afford readers a rich source of the enduring wisdom of mankind.

Sophia Institute Press makes high-quality books available to the general public by using advanced, cost-effective technology and by soliciting donations to subsidize general publishing costs. Your generosity can help us provide the public with editions of works containing the enduring wisdom of the ages. Send your tax-deductible contribution to the address noted below. Your questions, comments, and suggestions are also welcome.

For a free catalog, call:

Toll-Free: 1-800-888-9344

SOPHIA INSTITUTE PRESS
BOX 5284
MANCHESTER, NH 03108

Sophia Institute Press is a tax-exempt institution as defined by the Internal Revenue Service Code, Section 501(c)(3). Tax I.D. 22-2548708.